HOSTILE
INTENT

PROTECTING YOURSELF
FROM **TERRORISM**

HOSTILE
INTENT

PHIL LITTLE

WITH **ALBERT PERROTTA**

BROADMAN
&HOLMAN
PUBLISHERS

NASHVILLE, TENNESSEE

13-digit ISBN: 978-0-8054-4024-9
10-digit ISBN: 0-8054-4024-0

Published by Broadman & Holman Publishers,
Nashville, Tennessee

Dewey Decimal Classification: 303.6
Subject Headings: TERRORISM—UNITED STATES
                    EVANGELISTIC WORK
                    CURRENT EVENTS

Unless otherwise noted, Scripture quotations have been taken
from the Holman Christian Standard Bible®, Copyright © 1999,
2000, 2002, 2003 by Holman Bible Publishers.

1 2 3 4 5 6 7 8 9 10 09 08 07 06 05

Contents

Beginnings

"ANOTHER PROMISING DAY in the Promised Land," I blurted to George Otis, founder of High Adventure Ministries. It was a cool spring morning in Israel. The day before, we met with Israeli Prime Minister Menachem Begin. It hadn't been a social call; the tough and feisty leader was not one for idle chat. In fact, the former freedom fighter and future Nobel Prize winner was railing on the hardship being suffered by Christians in southern Lebanon, complaining with barely concealed contempt about how the Western world was looking the other way as the PLO invaded southern Lebanon, killing and driving families from their homes and cities. Begin issued us a challenge: "See for yourself. Go to southern Lebanon and meet Major Haddad, the leader of southern Lebanon." Both George and I liked living on the edge. Both trusted God to protect us, even in a war zone. And both wanted to avoid looking like wimps in front of Begin. "We accept!" And so, on this morning, we were on a collision course with destiny.

My First Taste of Terror

We were told to go to a small airport outside Tel Aviv, from which we would be flown to northern Israel, near the border with Lebanon. Anticipation had me bouncing like a puppy. Young, with a dash of would-be spy in me, I was too brash to consider the danger of entering a war zone where bullets and missiles were filling the air like mosquitoes, and I was too naive to comprehend how many of those missiles and bullets were intended for the man we were going to meet: Major Haddad.

We boarded a small, two-engined plane and were soon airborne . . . but not *too* airborne. The pilot, a fit and tan young man in civilian clothes, had us at quite a low altitude, no more than five thousand feet. "It's unsafe to fly higher because of the hostile conditions in the area, including possible missile firings." No need for an action movie on this flight. We watched the countryside go by, the beautiful colors of the ground below belying the deadly realities of war.

Suddenly, thirty minutes into our flight, we took a nosedive. I was no flying novice; in the U.S. Air Force, I'd landed in jet fighters at 150 miles per hour. But now my heart jumped into my throat, my mind loudly questioned the wisdom of this trip, and my lips could only manage something that sounded like "Whooaaaaahhh!" The pilot said we were near the landing strip though I could not see where. The plane kept screaming toward the ground in what I knew—absolutely—was too fast a descent. Then, with our mortal flesh only a few hundred feet off the ground, a small dirt strip appeared in front of us. *So* that's *where it was,* I remember thinking.

As the plane taxied to a stop and my heart returned to its proper place in my chest, a military jeep approached and stopped in front of us. Colonel Yourm, the liaison between Israel and southern Lebanon, jumped out and greeted us. During our introductions we discovered that our pilot was a military fighter jock. That explained the quick dive for the ground; he was accustomed to dodging missiles.

We were driven to Metulla, a small town near the border between Israel and Lebanon, and arrived at its only hotel. Although small, the Arrizme Hotel was large on intrigue. It was a virtual United Nations of espionage. Its fifty rooms were always at least half occupied by various spooks, all vying to determine or influence what was going to happen next in the region.

Today the village of Metulla has grown into a bustling town with hotels, restaurants, and a Canadian-built sports center. The facility is the largest sports center in this part of the world, providing high-quality sports and leisure activities. But in 1978, the leading sport and leisure activity was the spy game, and its center was the Arrizme Hotel.

Metulla is located between the biblical cities of Dan, Abel Beth Maacah, and Ijon in northern Israel. Aaron Edmond de Rothschild founded Metulla in 1896, and then helped immigrants from Russia settle the land. Metulla has experienced many hardships, but the grit of its residents has enabled them to grow a flourishing garden from a barren wasteland.

Looking to the east from the patio of the Arrizme, I saw Mount Hermon, dressed in white. The north and west offered a panoramic view of Metulla's position overlooking the Lebanese border and its use as the Israeli Northern Army headquarters. The high Lebanese mountains, also cloaked in white, overlooked Metulla from the north.

Today there is a museum in Metulla where one can learn the history of the settlement. But in 1978, I saw history being made before my own eyes. From the Arrizme Hotel, I saw the Israeli-Lebanese border and a chain-link fence with a gate known as the "Good Fence." As we waited for Major Haddad, I asked Colonel Yourm how the Good Fence got its name. "It's not the fence that's significant," he said. "It's the gate."

The Good Fence

A fence ran along the entire border between Israel and Lebanon, but the gate marked the start of a relationship between the citizens of two countries and symbolized Israel's humanitarian concern for the Lebanese. The story of the gate starts in 1976, when a desperate Lebanese mother came to the fence with her seriously ill son. The heart of an Israeli Defense Forces (IDF) soldier went out to the woman, and he helped her get treatment for the child. Shortly after, a critically wounded Lebanese also found treatment but died before he could return home. Word spread quickly about the kindness and care found at that spot, and the lines started forming early each morning: parents bringing their young children in hopes of a medical cure, soldiers wounded in battle, old people suffering from diseases and without any hope in Lebanon. The concern of one Israeli soldier—the love of one person for his neighbor—had ignited a relationship between two countries. Before long, a constant stream of Lebanese citizens was coming into northern Israel to work, play, and receive medical help. The Good Fence presented Israel to the world as an enlightened nation helping its northern neighbors who, though previously its enemies, were now engaged in a civil war whose end could not be predicted.

During those early days, the crossing was simply a crooked fence. All anyone had to do was crawl underneath to get to the other side. After awhile, a more official crossing was established near an IDF post, close to the apple orchards belonging to the residents of Metulla. A hut was set up. The hut turned into a clinic. The clinic turned into a cluster of buildings including waiting rooms and reception areas. A dirt road was built from the gate to the now flourishing medical center. And flying side by side over the medical center were the Israeli and Lebanese flags. Order and peace reigned over this one small corner of a troubled region, and nobody, not even the veteran Metulla residents, minded that this point on the uneasy border was turning into an attraction for tourists coming in by the thousands from all over the world. It took five years before the rest of the world caught wind of the Good Fence and Israel's passion and concern for the Lebanese people. But when the story did finally break in 1981, newspaper and TV reporters stampeded the area to send reports to Europe and America.

With the opening of the Good Fence, the northern frontier of Israel began to take on some of the characteristics of a normal border. Before 1976, there was no contact; it was a sealed border. But in those first five years, relations warmed considerably. In 1981 alone it was estimated that more than fifty thousand Lebanese visited Israel; and in the first four years after the opening of the Good Fence, Israeli doctors treated two hundred thousand patients. Sadly, all the while the Good Fence operated with Muslim, Christians, and Jews working together for the same cause—safety, peace, and a chance to raise their families—the PLO was continuing to build up its strength in southern Lebanon, making continual terrorist attacks on both the Lebanese Christians and the Israelis.

Unfortunately for all concerned, the media focused on the terrorist attacks and propaganda spewed by the PLO and its sympathizers and not on Israel's acts of compassion for its Lebanese neighbors. I can still picture the lines of mothers with sick children, the old who were barely able to make it to the gate, and Lebanese soldiers wounded by terrorists. Suddenly there was hope, and it came in the most unlikely place: from those the Lebanese had been told were their enemies. This was a story waiting to be told. Actually, it had been *foretold*. A sign at the Good Fence carried the words of the prophets Isaiah and Micah: "They will turn their swords into plows and their spears into pruning knives. Nations will not take up the sword against [other] nations, and they will never again train for war" (Isa. 2:4; Mic. 4:3).

Waiting for Major Haddad, the leader of southern Lebanon, gave me the opportunity to soak in the ancient atmosphere. We were at the crossroads of the world: where it all began and, if certain interpretations of biblical prophecies are true, where it will all end. I had a very strong sense that this was a special place. Despite the threat of war, I sensed a peaceful stillness. Listening closely to the wind, I could almost hear God himself whispering, "I am coming. Fear not."

As our wait for Major Haddad dragged on, it seemed God *would* arrive again before the major did. Was he even coming? Yes, we were told. Major Haddad's home had come under rocket fire, but we were to stay put. Eventually our waiting paid off: A line of five Lebanese jeeps approached the border, stopping at the Good Fence gate. When it opened, the jeeps sped through, halting in a cloud of dust in front of the hotel.

From one of the jeeps stepped a man in a dark-green baseball cap and a military uniform so crisp it appeared he had just come from the cleaners. He came toward us with the confident walk of a man in command, surrounded on all sides by uniformed soldiers of the southern Lebanese army with Uzis at the ready. This was Major Haddad. As we were introduced, his eyes locked onto mine. His gaze was clear blue, intense, and seemed to look deep into my soul. Instantly I knew this was a good man but one I would not want opposing me.

We spent the next two hours getting to know each other. George and I explained why we were in Israel. Major Haddad commented that there had been others from the United States who had come and said they were going to help; they soon left and were never heard from again. "Not even a postcard." He was concerned we would be the same old story: a lot of talk and no follow-through. George and I assured him we would help in any way we could.

Major Haddad and Colonel Yourm held a hushed discussion about taking us into Lebanon. They debated the dangers, informing us that Major Haddad also had been delayed by PLO rockets fired at his jeeps from Beufort Castle. Overlooking the Litani River, Beufort Castle offers a bird's-eye view of northern Israel. The PLO had taken over the castle, giving it a perfect perch for firing missiles into Israel and targeting those traveling nearby roads. "We're up for it!" we insisted. George and I love adventure and weren't about to miss the opportunity to go into Lebanon. Little did we know our exciting little fling was destined to become a long-term commitment.

Under the Guns of Beufort Castle

WE LOADED INTO THE five jeeps and headed for the border. The Good Fence gate swung open, and we accelerated through. I was sure I could hear the James Bond theme in the roar of the engines. Soon we were racing along a narrow road, which, like most roads in southern Lebanon, was paved only with dirt and was in dire need of repair. And the roads weren't all that needed fixing; the first town we came to had been a city of forty thousand people. Yet as we drove through the streets there wasn't a soul to be seen. Every building was empty. Additionally, each building was pocked with countless shell holes, every window was broken, and most doors were off the hinges. Hopelessness hung everywhere, even on the soldiers with us. We continued into other towns and villages, finding more of the same: bullet holes and abandoned towns. As we drove rapidly across the ridge overlooking the Litani River, I got my first glimpse of Beufort Castle on the far bluff, a thousand feet above the rushing Litani. From this distance, it looked like a toy, but through field glasses I could make out details of the imposing and seemingly impenetrable fortress, with walls six feet thick, set on the mountain.

A Ride in the War Zone

We stopped on the ridge road to take a closer look. The castle has been called "impenetrable Beufort." The more than a dozen other Crusader castles in Lebanon cannot compare with Beufort in size, scenic grandeur, or close connection with Lebanese history down to modern times. What I was looking at from the ridge on the other side of the Litani River was less a picturesque medieval ruin than a rock pile obscuring broken towers and battlements. The defensive mass of buildings was mostly underground.

In the powerful field glasses I could see the massive castle entrance. The fortress was made of huge, chiseled blocks of granite and had a sunken archway entrance. When closed and barred, it would stand indefinitely against the most devout attackers. Now the fort was under control of the PLO, which used its commanding position to mercilessly pound northern Israel and southern Lebanon and its underground vaults to store munitions and weapons out of reach of Israeli rockets. Across the tops of the broken walls and towers, Petrushka rockets and other missiles of destruction could be quickly moved into place and launched at any target that caught the eye.

Apparently, we caught the PLO's eye.

As I stood admiring the view, I heard a soldier yell, "Look out!" A rocket, trailing smoke and vapor, was racing from the castle toward our position. *Neat!* I thought, not moving. It took awhile to grasp the concept that a rocket fired directly at me could be hazardous to my health. A soldier grabbed me by the shoulder and flung me like a rag into a jeep as a second soldier hit the gas and sped us off the ridge. Seconds later, a ferocious blast cracked the air behind us. I turned in time to see a ball of orange fire rising from a spot roughly one hundred yards from where we had been standing. Fortunately, the PLO's aim is even worse than its animosity.

"The PLO didn't like us stopping and viewing the castle," a soldier explained. The PLO also knew the caravan contained the man at the top of its hit list: Major Haddad, a man it tried to kill at every opportunity. In fact, when our relationship with Major Haddad became known, we, too, found our way onto the PLO hit list. But I'm getting ahead of the story.

As we raced along the ridge road, our jeeps kept playing leapfrog. The lead jeep would slow, and the one behind would pass and take the lead. A little farther along, the third jeep would hop to the front. I knew from my military and police days that this was a diversion designed to confuse the terrorists in Beufort Castle who were targeting Major Haddad's jeep. It was a life-or-death shell game—*shell* being the operative word. We kept up the tactic until we reached the major's village, Marjayoun.

Marjayoun, whose proper name is Jedaidat Marjayoun, has produced many distinguished Lebanese immigrants, including America's first jet ace, Maj. James Jabara of Korean War fame. Today, it's known for being the largest Lebanese town in the south Beqaa Valley, the district headquarters, and the market center of the region. Sitting on a hill, Marjayoun was a perfect location for an army outside guarding a portion of the Palestinian frontier. This strategic location was Major Haddad's home and his military headquarters. His forces gained control of the region before my arrival in 1978, having driven the PLO back north of the Litani River. Still, they remained susceptible to missiles and other terrorist attacks by the PLO.

This was instantly evident as we pulled up in front of a simple house on a small street. The first thing I noticed was layer upon layer of sandbags circling the house. The next thing I noticed was a tiny two-year-old girl with long, curly hair and the biggest brown eyes. My heart immediately went out to her. She was Major Haddad's youngest daughter, and as I've watched her grow up over the years, her child's face remains the one memory I always cherish about that first visit to Lebanon. She led us into her house and down into the basement, where the family was forced to spend most of the time, thanks to persistent shelling by the PLO. The terrorists wanted Major Haddad dead and didn't care who they killed to get him, even that precious little two-year-old.

The major's wife served us very sweet coffee in little cups, accompanied by small, very sugary rolls. One cup of the coffee was enough to make me sit up straight and politely refuse a refill. Over the coffee, Major Haddad described his people's difficult circumstances. "How can we help?" we asked. "I can't talk with my people," he replied, referring to the one hundred and twenty-five thousand residents of southern or free Lebanon. "I'd like to have a small transmitter, perhaps five to ten thousand watts, just enough to cover the ten by thirty miles of southern Lebanon." While he was envisioning a small mobile transmitter that could be set up in his office, the seed of something much bigger began to stir inside our imaginations—not that we knew the first thing about building a radio station of any size.

We were drawn into the life and family of Major Haddad. The more he talked of the hardship and daily threat to his people's existence, the stronger we felt about becoming part of the solution. During the next two hours, we heard the heart of this man who had put his life, his army career, and his family on the line to save his country. With each word we were more convinced of his passion and vision for rescuing Lebanon and driving the terrorists from his homeland. Major Haddad recalled how, when the PLO entered Lebanon, it moved into the mostly Christian south on a systematic death march from town to village, slaughtering those Lebanese citizens who did not leave. The PLO methods were brutal, preying on men, women, and children alike. Here was a genocidal onslaught before such euphemistic phrases as "ethnic cleansing" came into being. Major Haddad was in the regular Lebanese army stationed in Beirut when the PLO made its entry into south Lebanon. The south was lightly defended, making it easy for the PLO to roam freely. Major Haddad and others tried to get support from the government in Beirut to stop the slaughter, but because of Syrian influence and the fact that the south was Christian, military support was blocked. As the PLO gained control of southern Lebanon, it began to use the region as a launching point for attacks on Israel. Later, we'll see this as the start of what would be the PLO's downfall. As we examine the history of terror we'll learn that time after time, the terrorists, by increasing the level and intensity of the violence, have brought about their own destruction.

The attacks were being waged with rockets aimed at northern Israel, raining down night after night. Life in northern Israel was dangerous, and Israeli impatience with the Lebanese government's inaction quickly turned into action. They started striking back with F-15s and attack helicopters, with the initial goal being to halt the nightly attacks on northern Israel. The Israelis soon found that when they destroyed one camp, another sprang to life the next day. The PLO used its people as if they were expendable and without value, fodder to be ground up in the name of conquest.

The Israeli government decided the only way to stop the attacks was to have a buffer zone along its northern border with Lebanon. This was a radical change in policy. It meant Israel would now have to invade another country, which, of course, guaranteed the Jewish state a whole host of additional problems. However, the option of inaction meant the continued slaughter of its innocent citizens, and thus the decision to take stronger military action was made. Israel did not want to occupy southern Lebanon, so it set out to find Lebanese citizens they could assist with training and weapons to pick up the fight to protect southern Lebanon. Major Haddad soon came to light as someone Israel could work with. He had walked away from his career and had returned to Marjayoun to fight the PLO. His stand made the major a wanted man in the eyes of the Lebanese government. But a shared desire to see the PLO pushed away from the Israeli border pulled Israel and Major Haddad into an unlikely partnership.

Apathy and Politics: An Unholy Alliance

It's hard to imagine a country allowing a foreign army, even a nonuniformed one, to take control without a fight. However, when we consider that Syria has historically considered Lebanon a part of a greater Syria and has always meddled in Lebanese affairs, the picture becomes clearer. Syria was looking for avenues to strike at Israel without suffering retaliatory attacks on Syrian soil; Lebanon proved to be a perfect front for such a strategy. Syria's grip on the Lebanese government was so tight it was able to help the PLO take control of southern Lebanon and do what it wished with the mostly Christians locals, who were, in Syria's view, expendable because of their faith.

The stories haunt me to this day. In 1977 a local mayor who stood up to the PLO was dragged to the center of town where thugs tied a rope to each of his legs and arms. They then attached the ropes to four vehicles. The vehicles roared off in different directions, ripping the mayor to pieces. Men were killed in front of their wives and children to frighten other families into leaving. Executions were carried out in town squares with horrified communities looking on. This very public and brutal campaign accomplished its purpose: It destroyed the will of the people who saw no one coming to their aid. Not only had their own government deserted them, but the rest of the world was strangely silent. I continue to be amazed at this silence, in contrast to the outcry that often occurs when Palestinians are wounded while challenging the Israeli army as it tries to protect Israeli citizens from those who wish them harm.

We were sitting in the middle of a historical time bomb. We could see the Valley of the Springs and Mount Hermon in the distance, as well as Megiddo, the very place named in Revelation as the location of the last great battle. Our minds were racing, envisioning a voice crying out from the Valley of the Springs that not only would speak to southern Lebanon but perhaps to the whole Middle East.

Perhaps we should have asked ourselves some questions, thought through some of the logistics. We would need Israel's support to import the equipment and build a radio station. Would Israel allow this? What would Israelis think of a Christian radio station on their border, broadcasting into their country? Yes, this could be an opportunity that only comes once in a lifetime, but could we accomplish it? Where would we get the funds and the technical support to design the station? And what did we know about building and operating a radio station, anyway?

However, these questions and many, many others evaporated in the emotional heat of the moment and the passion of Major Haddad. Besides, when George Otis locks into a God-vision, he tears into it like a bulldog, going anywhere and to anybody for help and not taking no for an answer. His determination and focus certainly rubbed off on me.

My mind and spirit were racing, moved and thrilled by the feeling that I had been cast in a real-life action adventure as intense as any of the movie thrillers of my youth—except the sandbags around the house were real, the machine guns in the corner had actual bullets, and the missiles fired at us had live warheads. I didn't experience any fear. Given later events and increased wisdom, perhaps I should have. Instead, that day I was ready to spring into action.

Action came quickly, thanks to Major Haddad. He looked into my eyes and asked a question reminiscent of Acts 16:9: "Will you come over and help us?" Seeing into the heart and soul of the man, I knew I was ready right then to pick up an Uzi and do battle at his side. What else was I to say in the face of such a call from this man who had been raised up for such a time as this? We had not a moment's hesitation. We left his sandbagged basement vowing to him that we would go back to the States and begin working on constructing a radio station for that tear-soaked soil.

Darkness was falling as we left his home for the journey back across the ridge, under the guns of Beufort Castle. We were told it would be safer in the darkness since it would be harder for the PLO to effectively target us. As our jeep caravan moved across the ridge above the Litani River, we could see the streaking flash of rockets being fired at northern Israel. Each meteor of death reinforced our commitment to help, and not only with the radio station. The people of southern Lebanon needed medical and school supplies along with other support to rebuild their economic structure.

Crossing through the Good Fence into Israel was like crossing into another world. We had gone from dirt roads, bullet-riddled towns, and stores without the basic necessities to a thriving town with paved streets, fully-stocked stores, and bustling restaurants. But the most noticeable difference was the people. In Israel, the people had hope on their faces. They were smiling, even though they lived under the constant threat of war. In

Lebanon, the people rarely smiled or looked at anyone. The sense of doom and hopelessness saturated the air and land.

Back at the hotel, George and I talked about what we had seen, heard, and learned. But instead of feeling despair or setting ourselves to go back to America and get on with our lives, Major Haddad's request still rang in our ears: "Will you come over and help us?" We would not, could not, ignore the call. *Will you come over and help us?* Yes, but could our abilities meet his needs? *Will you come over and help us?* "We can do it!" exclaimed George. "We can build them a radio station!"

We were invited to stay in Metulla and spend some time with the military and political leaders of the area. Before long we were in the home command post of the officer in charge of the region. It reminded me of a set for a war movie; field radios were cranking out reports about where the missiles were falling and then detailing casualties. I was watching and listening to conversations about troop movements and army strategies.

Our hosts didn't really know us, but they seemed to be comfortable with us listening in. What had they been told about us? Had the prime minister's office called the commander with background information on George and me? I knew that George's High Adventure Ministries was well known as a friend of Israel, and George himself was a vocal supporter of Israel in the States. But with my background in investigations and intelligence, I was more accustomed to the "need-to-know" approach. Still, it made me feel important to be trusted.

My ears perked up when I heard talk about movement along the border; terrorists were trying to cross that no-man's-land, a strip of sand fenced on both sides with lights and sensors. A few would make it across, but most would be detected and tracked down before they got to any of the towns in Israel. Only occasionally would one elude the determined Israeli army and deliver death and destruction to unsuspecting civilians. This was my first glimpse of the massive security job facing the Israelis, just on their northern border—only a fraction of the daily defense issues the nation deals with.

Take, for example, terrorist training camps. The PLO and other terrorist organizations were and are using refugee camps as covers for their training facilities. They can hide in the middle of thousands of people, reducing the risk of retaliatory strikes. Israel, with its respect for life, is hesitant to endanger the civilians the PLO uses as shields. The strategy also helps camouflage foreigners who come for training.

Records recovered from the camps have proven to contain many names and addresses from the United States. A chill went over me as I looked down the list of my fellow citizens, with names like Williams, Johnson, Abrams, some with addresses in southern California, within striking distance of my family and friends. What could drive a person to come all this way to live in the squalid conditions of the camps to learn how to kill their fellow Americans? Surprise turned to outrage. Why hadn't we heard of this before? Why were so many in our government and country supporting the PLO and their training regime of death? This story had to be told; and I was convinced that if the American people were told the truth, they would rise up and demand our government do something to stop this deadly plot against Americans and our way of life. At that very moment, I vowed to myself that I would learn all I could about terrorism, the Middle East, the PLO and its connections, and how we could keep America safe.

The many horrors perpetrated by the PLO in butchering innocent people were only a fraction of the story. Over time, I would learn the terrorists' barbaric behavior was part of a bigger scheme. The PLO was training fighters not to recapture a homeland. They planned to export terrorism out of the Middle East with America as the ultimate target. The overriding mission was and is to impose their brand of religion on the rest of us, and they had the permission of their god to use violence to achieve their purpose. This is alien and difficult to understand for us in the West who know a God of love and a religion of nonviolence. I was being rudely awakened to the fight we had before us and the depths of evil to which our enemy had descended. September 11 was still nearly twenty-five years away, but my education on world terrorism was opening my eyes to the harsh realization that such a day would come.

My New Calling

George and I prepared to leave Israel. Our hosts asked us about our plans. Were we coming back to the region? We discussed the meeting we had with Major Haddad and his request for a "little" radio station to communicate with his people. We told the Israelis we were going to help, but, we asked, "How in the world are we going to get the equipment into Lebanon?" "No problem," the Israeli officials said. "Our army will assist with the logistics." Israel recognized that any help we could give to Major Haddad was in its own national interest. True enough, as we began building the station, Israel came to our aid time and time again, unlike our own government.

As we walked out of the commander's home on the way to our own home country, we again saw the streaks of light and fire—rockets spewing from Beufort Castle. *Every night they have to deal with this,* I thought, amazed and humbled. On the ride back to Tel Aviv we began laying our plans for the station. But in my own mind, a new vision began coming into focus: I was going to put in place a world-class intelligence-gathering and research group to help expose the evil behind the face of the PLO. Even as I was leaving, I was already planning my return to this historic and holy place, prayerfully preparing for the world-changing, spirit-challenging situations awaiting me in the Promised Land.

"Send me," the prophet Isaiah told the Lord, "send me." I felt the call deep in my soul.

Shout of Terror

ALL WE COULD THINK or talk about during our final two days in Israel was our clandestine meeting at Major Haddad's home and the plans for the radio station. The thought of having a voice in the Middle East was almost too much for George to contain. His mind was already racing at full speed, and I was scrambling to catch up. We started scratching out preliminary lists of things we thought needed to be done to get the radio station project rolling. Our twelve-hour flight home was consumed with the question of how to build the thing.

Back in Los Angeles, my time was quickly swallowed up by briefings on detective agency concerns. Still, as I settled back into the daily routine, my thoughts were increasingly filled with images of Lebanon and the horror being brought against her people. How could I make a difference despite being so far away? I began to see the glimmer of a possible answer. First, I would gather all the information I could on the terrorists. Second, I would present that information before the American people in every forum possible. I would expose the growing terrorist threat. Would my friends in international intelligence and law enforcement help?

Before I had time to organize a plan of action, George was scheduling our next trip back to Lebanon. We were quickly discovering that we couldn't merely toss together a radio station; we needed to know a lot of data about the land, the airwaves, where we intended to place the station, and a thousand other technical questions. And hanging over everything we did was the likelihood that anything we built would be attacked by Palestinian terrorists. It was like being enrolled in Building a Radio Station in a War Zone 101, and there wasn't even a text-book. After a few weeks, George said he was heading back and taking a specialist with him to determine the best frequencies for the area. He wanted me to go too. It took me less than a second to agree because I was eager to be part of a world-changing effort. I also was driven by a love of adventure and a desire to learn all I could about terrorism. If I was going to successfully build a counterterrorism organization, I would need all the up-to-date information I could get my hands on. And what better place to do that than at the wellspring of terrorism?

As naive as we were about radio station building, we were equally naive about politics. We actually assumed that President Carter's State Department would support our effort to help the people of Lebanon. We started making contacts in Washington, and instead of the expected "Go get 'em! Atta boy!" we were slapped in the face with "What are you zealots doing? You're out of your league! You're messing with foreign policy!" I can still hear the red-faced State Department official ordering us at the top of his lungs, "Stay out of Lebanon!" Our accounts of the PLO's genocide against the Lebanese didn't make a dent in their minds. There's no diplomatic way to say it: The Carter State Department was more interested in foreign policy niceties than in saving lives. Supporting the PLO, no matter what it did, seemed to be the order of the day. So, instead of waiting use-lessly, trying to convince a government that didn't want to hear what we had to say, we decided to move forward with all haste. With the ethnic cleansing in Lebanon continuing unabated, we realized speed was our order of the day, along with keeping a low profile.

Within days we were on a plane to Israel with radio specialist Paul Hunter and tower construction expert Stormy Weathers in tow. Stormy Weathers—yes, that's his real name—owned an antenna business in Oklahoma and was offering to build our antennas.

Surveying a Dream

The pull of Israel is strong, echoing the yearning and prayer at the end of each Passover meal: "Next year in Jerusalem." And like the Israelites of old, I returned with a sense of purpose and homecoming—*homecoming* because it was a land I knew and loved so well from Scripture and *purpose* because I knew I was there for a job: to offer my skills and sweat to help protect the innocent from the evils of terrorism. I had seen the faces of the suffering in Lebanon and could not escape the prophets' command to care for the "widows and orphans."

Despite tight security at Tel Aviv's airport, we breezed through baggage claim and out the terminal without being stopped or searched. Israeli profilers must have given us a thumbs-up. We were met by a great friend of High Adventure; I'll call him Isaac. In addition to helping us, he was also doing a lot of government and military groundwork in Israel. He was to be our door opener, continually preparing the way for us.

Thanks to Isaac, the command on the northern front knew we were coming and had already issued clearances for us to go into Lebanon whenever we needed to. Arriving at the northern front, we checked back into my favorite spy hotel, the Arrizme. There we met Col. Yoram Hamizrachi for dinner, to discuss our plans for building the radio station. "I'll let Major Haddad know you're here," he said. "You'll be able to meet with him and go into Lebanon tomorrow." We then discussed the placement of the transmitter towers. "How about putting the tower and studio in Israel?" we asked the colonel. No-go, he told us. The Israelis would fully back a station in Lebanon, but it would be impossible to place an evangelical Christian station on Israeli soil. It was Lebanon or nothing. That night I went to sleep with thoughts of the spies in the rooms around me and what they might be planning. I have quite an active imagination.

I was up at dawn the next morning with the excitement of a seven-year-old heading to Disneyland. I bounded out of the hotel, pulling in the fresh air and gazing at the towering peaks of Mount Hermon. But while sipping coffee at the outdoor café, I was overwhelmed by the importance of the very ground I was standing on. *How much longer can this part of the world sustain all the hate forced on it?* A voice stilled my soul: "'Be strong, all you people of the land'—the LORD's declaration. 'Work! For I am with you'—the declaration of the LORD of Hosts" (Hag. 2:4b).

Major Haddad and his bodyguards arrived at 9:00 a.m., and over breakfast we discussed our itinerary. Our first order of business would be selecting a location for our radio tower. We had two things to consider: where to get the best signal and how to keep the terrorists from destroying it. Major Haddad confirmed that the station would immediately become a target of the PLO once it was built, so we had to consider security issues for whatever location we selected. Sounding more like a real estate agent than a military leader, Major Haddad said, "I have some places for you to look at, and then you can make a decision."

As our convoy rolled through the Good Fence gate, my excitement was wrestling with my fear. We had been warned that PLO patrols were making swift incursions as far south as they could, sometimes targeting the roads we'd be on, killing anyone they ran into. My fear was eased, though, by the presence of Haddad's well-armed soldiers.

We went to several different locations, but each posed a host of security issues, mostly to do with the proximity of Beufort Castle. Finally, the major announced, "I have one last location for us to look at. It's back near the Israeli border checkpoint." I wondered why we didn't go there first; it seemed that the closer to the border we built, the better. We drove back and descended into the Valley of the Springs, just a little more than a mile from the Good Fence. Dropping down over a ridge put us completely out of sight of Beufort Castle. As we hopped out of the jeeps and began surveying the land, we begin to sense that this was God's location. Paul, our frequency expert, began taking his readings and within an hour proclaimed, "This is perfect." The major then pointed out a nearby building that could house our transmitters and generators. A brief drive away, he stopped at another building. "You can have this for your studio," he said, again the real estate agent. I snapped picture after picture. They'd prove useful in developing a security plan to protect the station and its American and Lebanese staff. We then circled the buildings in prayer, staking claim to this piece of land, and calling on the Lord's protection to keep it safe.

Of course, finding a place for the station was the easy part. The heavy lifting would come with raising money to build the station and exporting the equipment from the United States while avoiding the scrutiny of the State Department. A piece of cake for a bunch of novices? Sometimes inexperience is an ally. Sometimes one is selected for a job that the experienced would look at and say, "This is too difficult and dangerous," then turn away. Major Haddad knew this all too well. People from the States had come to him with their plans, ideas, and best intentions. But they'd take one look at the war zone, say, "No, thank you," and fly home. These were men who had experience at building radio stations. The difference with us? We didn't know all the reasons we couldn't do it. We just knew if God was in it, a way would be made. David's brothers weren't cowardly when they looked across the field and saw Goliath licking his chops; they only thought they were being realistic.

In addition to the green light from God and my gung-ho naïveté, I also felt in my spirit that helping build the station would be critical to the forging of my counterterrorist organization and my relationship with Israel. So before we left the property, we gathered around Major Haddad, took his hand, and made a vow: "This station will be built." Driving back to the border, we enjoyed the beautiful countryside; the calm of the day seemed to thumb its nose at the hostiles lurking over the next hill.

Back at the Arrizme, we met with Israeli military leaders and shared what we had accomplished. They were supportive and eager to help. Eager to get myself in the middle of the action, I finagled an invitation to join the military commanders for dinner in hopes of picking their brains. I wanted to find out all I could about terrorist groups and, in particular, what the Israelis knew about the training camps and their operations. I needed the full story if I was going to be effective in proving to Americans the real purpose of the terrorists.

The Inside Story

The Israelis' story began with a chilling account of evil forces from different backgrounds coming together at the camps in Lebanon, unifying under a mission to change the world through hate and violence. Remember, the Cold War was at its height and the United States was in a staring match with the Soviet Union. The Soviets were using any means necessary to destabilize the United States, and they found a perfect ally in the radical terrorists driven by centuries of hatred for Jews. Because the United States supported Israel, we were seen by militant Muslims as the Great Satan preventing them from defeating their enemy. The Soviets were masters at using surrogates and getting others to do their dirty work—techniques currently used by Iran and Syria. They were also in a position to meet some of the terrorists' most important needs, such as training, arms, and the transportation of documents and weapons under diplomatic cover. Both parties thought they were smarter than the other. The Soviets thought they could use the Arab terrorists and then control them, while the terror groups thought they would use the Soviets and then toss them aside. This was the climate in southern Lebanon in the 1970s: the Soviets and Arab terror groups tag-teaming to target American and Israeli interests.

The Soviets had maintained military advisers in Syria for some time. Many of these people were actually intelligence officers specializing in urban warfare and terrorist tactics. They had been in and out of Lebanon as guests of the Syrians for years before the PLO moved in. Now their interest was doubled because of the hatred of the PLO and other terrorist groups toward the United States. Their motto was "The enemy of my enemy is my friend." The records we recovered prove not only the Soviet Union's presence at leadership meetings of the terrorists, but the extent to which the Soviets offered advice and support. We had communications intercepts of meetings in which they discussed sending terrorists to train at the model American towns set up by the Soviets so terrorists could better infiltrate the American population. The Soviets also offered forged passports and other travel documents so a terrorist could hide his true country of origin. The Soviets encouraged attacks on Western interests, particularly those of the United States. Minutes from the meetings indicate the terrorists' one obsession was figuring out how to get at the continental United States, despite our being surrounded by friends and water. The terror groups held heated strategy meetings about U.S. intelligence and our (then) strong, preventive approach to law enforcement. The terrorist leadership determined that they had to work to tear down this aspect of our defenses before successful attacks could penetrate our borders. They already had an offensive under way to break down the defenses of Europe through propaganda; specifically, they claimed that law enforcement in those countries was being used to spy on citizens and violate their rights (an ironic claim, given the Soviet government's approach to the rights of its citizens). Events of the '70s and '80s in Europe demonstrated, for anyone willing to see, the destructive effectiveness of this disinformation onslaught. They almost got away with it.

As I listened to the reports and read the record, I recognized the distant drumbeat beginning to sound in Los Angeles. The American Civil Liberties Union and other leftist organizations had started an assault on the Los Angeles Police Department, claiming that its intelligence unit was spying on the public and should be disbanded. An alarm went off inside my head: *The destabilization program is already under way in the U.S.!* Further, the Olympics were coming to Los Angeles in 1984, and all we would need was one major terrorist attack to change the course of our freedom. Realizing a plan of destabilization not unlike the tactics used by the Soviets and their terrorist allies was already at work on our shores made me doubly committed to action. The Israelis made the point to me over and over that the only way to stop the terrorists was to have good information on what they're planning, then prevent their attack. Evidently, I needed to learn more about what the bad guys were doing in Europe. Armed with that information, I could wake up and enlist the American people to stop the politicians from destroying preventive law enforcement. The Israelis encouraged me to become a voice crying out danger, like the prophets of old warning of impending doom if the people didn't change their actions.

These early meetings in Israel got me acquainted with the European terrorist groups; they had all been trained by Soviets in camps in southern Lebanon. I also learned that many of the attacks carried out in Europe were planned and executed from Lebanon. Standard operating procedure would include leaving Beirut early in the morning traveling on false passports, preferably from a European country. They'd fly to France or Italy, detonate their bombs, and be back in Beirut by dinner. Following their trail was no easy task; for the next time they traveled, they'd use a different passport with a different name. We were up against very motivated and committed people who were good at what they did. Unfortunately, their motivation and commitment haven't flagged through the years. If we're going to beat them, we have to become as committed and motivated in our defense strategies.

That evening, after my time with the Israeli military leaders, I had a lot on my mind. I stared at the ceiling in my hotel room. *This is too big for me. Who am I to think anyone will listen to me? How can I develop a plan to expose the terrorists' purposes when they have so many powerful people and the gullible media on their side?* Then my upbringing kicked in. I heard my mother's sweet, assuring voice: "Remember who you are. You have the God of heaven on your side." My spirit eased, and a sense of divine peace settled over me as I drifted off to a restful sleep.

The Voice of Hope Is Born

GEORGE'S DREAM WAS to broadcast the message of salvation over the airwaves throughout the Middle East, and he was determined to figure out how to make that happen. In his mind, he had already named our radio station project the Voice of Hope. He and Paul Hunter decided that because we were there anyway we should do frequency checks on the drive back to Jerusalem, in case we had a future opportunity to put repeating stations in Israel. By noon, we were motoring south, stopping first above the Sea of Galilee. I was walking where Jesus walked. Today I'm awed by the memory, but that day our immediate concern was whether we were attracting any attention by pulling off the road and setting up instruments. What would the locals think? More important, what would they do? Would we be mistaken for terrorists planting a bomb or guiding a remote device? Fortunately, none of our half-dozen stops on the way to Jerusalem was eventful. We attracted some open stares, but thankfully we weren't stopped or questioned.

Back in Jerusalem we met up with Isaac, our local friend who was to become the point person for building the station. Isaac was the kind of guy who grew on me, and, over time, he moved from being an associate to becoming a member of the family. Whenever Isaac, his wife, and kids would visit LA, the little house took on the raucous air of a family reunion. Sending him off at the airport came to feel like saying good-bye to a close brother.

We developed a plan of action for covering our needs in Israel: Isaac would get cracking on the local logistics while we returned home to raise money and look for equipment. We now had a tangible sense that this station was really going to happen. People and things were falling in line, and momentum was starting to build.

Once again, we were giddy and productive on the flight back to Los Angeles, scribbling out lists of all the people we wanted to draw into the project financially, technically, logistically, and spiritually. We still had no idea of what we were getting into. If we had, we might have taken the same round trip as the pros who had considered this earlier. But isn't that just like Jehovah, to enlist a bunch of amateurs without the baggage of knowing what the world says is impossible? For example, what would a harp-twanging shepherd know about being a king? What does a fisherman know about building a church? What does an LA gumshoe know about building a radio tower? We just thought, *Wow! Great opportunity! Let's do it!* We weren't thinking about how to get a one-hundred-thousand-dollar transmitter out of the United States, through Israel, and into the dangerous war zone of Lebanon, or how to get all the pieces of a two-hundred-foot tower through customs in Israel, truck it north across the border, and then actually erect it in Lebanon with terrorists looking on. Nor were we considering how far our own State Department would go, how ruthless it would be, in attempting to sabotage our project. As I look back, I thank God we didn't know any of this, or we might have given up before we started. But this was too big to stop. "Why on earth did you pick us?" we sometimes ask God. "Because," he answers, "you were willing."

After getting back to the States, I couldn't get out of my mind all I had learned from Israel's Mossad antiterrorist group on the methods the terrorists and Soviets were using to tear down our defenses and implode the democracies of the world. Keeping my ear to the ground, I could hear the whispering of the radicals in Los Angeles, starting their attacks on preventive law enforcement. It was as if I were reading straight from the playbook the terrorists had laid out in their meetings in Lebanon. The rhetoric was the same, almost to the syllable. The story written in the terrorist camps was being acted out in front of my local news cameras. From our then-headquarters on the corner of Union and Olympic, I'd look out at the high-rise buildings of downtown Los Angeles, wondering, *What can I do? I am only one person, and who will listen to me?* And always God's Spirit would respond: "Where is a man that will stand in the gap; one who will sound the alarm?"

My investigation discovered that Europe was aflame, with some countries paralyzed almost to the point that it wasn't safe for people to go to the bank or market because of indiscriminate terrorist attacks. My thirst grew to learn all I could about how terrorist operatives had gained their foothold in Europe. I amassed data and background on groups such as the Red Brigade in Italy, the ETA in Spain, Action Directe in France, the Red Army Faction in Germany, and the IRA in Ireland. Unknown to most Americans even today, these groups all had a common DNA: They were trained in Lebanon and had been infiltrated by Middle Eastern groups and the Soviets. They were being encouraged and supported in the hope they could create enough chaos across Europe to cause democratic governments to destabilize and fall. Their main rallying cry in the press—and through their sympathetic surrogates—was, "The government is spying on the people. Take away their intelligence-gathering and preventive measures!" In other words, they demanded the elimination of the very measures that had held the terrorists in check.

Unbelievably, it was working. Many of the countries of Europe were meekly dismantling their most effective units. Could this happen in the United States—right here in Los Angeles? After seeing how effective the terrorist approach had been in Europe and how quickly the radical argument was beginning to carry the day in LA, I was not convinced we would be any smarter than our hapless European neighbors.

Meanwhile, George was busy putting together the pieces of Voice of Hope. It wasn't long until we had the transmitter and tower lined up. Now we just had to get them to Lebanon and— oh, one minor problem—raise the money to pay for them. George's pit-bull mentality kicked in, and he started contacting everyone he knew and even more he didn't—anyone who might be remotely interested in our effort. Soon the funds started coming in. George planned another trip back to Lebanon to work on the logistics of shipping the equipment overseas and into the Valley of the Springs. I had my hands full in Los Angeles, but we agreed I'd support him from stateside.

Staring at the world map spread across one full wall of my office, I could easily get lost in a daydream; the bright colors and names of exotic cities transported me to Madrid, Vienna, Rome, and beyond. In my overactive imagination, I was a superspy gliding in and out of Paris as the master Soviet agent Natasha tried to seduce me and learn all my secrets. "Phil . . . Phil . . . ." As I surfaced from my mental vacation from reality I realized that, instead of the sultry voice of Natasha, it was the stern voice of my assistant: "Phil, there's a man asking for you. He'll only say he was referred by a friend." I have a lot of friends, but sometimes people calling a detective agency don't want to give out their names. Naturally, I was curious about who'd be on the other end of the phone. "How may I help you?" I said.

The voice on the other end sounded nice—almost grand-fatherly. "We haven't met," he said, "but we should." This sounded intriguing. The mysterious gentleman went on to say he had learned of my involvement in the Middle East, particu-larly southern Lebanon, and that he had a similar interest. Now I became cautious. As a rule, I trod very carefully when some-one started talking about sensitive matters in which I was involved. However, with assorted elements, particularly those in our own State Department, trying to shut us down before we got off the ground, I was on even higher alert. We sparred back and forth on the phone until Mr. X finally told me the agency he was with and offered his phone number, along with the name of an FBI contact who could verify his identity. "Go ahead and check me out," he said. "Then I'd like to meet and talk about our shared interest in stopping terrorists." Having been transplanted to California from Missouri—the Show-Me State—I took him up on his offer. "I'll do some checking and get back to you," I said. Within half an hour, I had determined Mr. X was who he claimed and called him back. The operator answered with the name of the agency he had provided. This wasn't proof because that can be easily faked, but I also hadn't been greeted by the waitress at some local pizza joint. At the very least, Mr. X was thorough. Earl (not his real name) sug-gested we meet in a downtown hotel lobby. I agreed, and thus started a long relationship with a man and mentor whose heart pounded with the same passion as mine for our country and our world.

During these early meetings with my new friend, my desire to build an international intelligence organization took practical form. Earl offered critical insight into developing and operating such a unit: insight gained from his many years on the ground. I absorbed a lot about the tradecraft of intelligence gathering from

Earl through long conversations about his past exploits and how he had survived his years in the field. Later, when faced with decisions that could very well mean life or death, the lessons from Earl literally saved me.

I told Earl all that I had gathered on the ground in Lebanon and Israel; I related my concern that there were forces already at work in our country and even in Los Angeles that would increase our vulnerability to terrorism. I confessed my internal battle over which direction I should go in trying to make a practical differ-ence. I didn't have any political experience or contacts of any importance in the city government, I admitted, and didn't know how to make those contacts.

Most people who met me back then assumed I was really out-going and not intimidated by anyone or anything. How little they knew. Still, after listening to my concerns, Earl encouraged me and gave me a quick lesson on making political contacts and getting my voice heard. In addition, he stuffed my files with a bounty of background material on the European terrorist groups, the political climate in those countries, and how the ter-rorists used surrogates to pressure governments to dismantle pre-ventive law enforcement. How troubling to see the methods of the overseas terrorists in the crazy actions of American radicals. Every day in Los Angeles the headlines screamed, "Police Unit Spies on the Public"; day after day, the cry got louder for the city to disband the intelligence unit. I cringed as ACLU-represented groups, such as the Communist Workers Party and individuals from the left, whose agenda was nothing less than the overthrow of the U.S. government continued pressing their claims in the media and in the courts. There was not one voice defending the police or standing up to these radical voices seeking to destroy our way of life.

Making Connections

Finally, one morning I mustered the courage to call the city council office in my district. I got my councilman on the phone, and I had barely begun to explain the reason for my call when he blurted, "Where have you people been?" *You people?* "We have dozens of radicals coming to the council testifying that we don't need intelligence gathering, and not one person has come to state the other side," he said. After listening to me share my concerns for a few minutes, he said—actually, it was closer to an order— "Get involved! Get your voice heard! Come before the council and tell what you've learned!"

I hung up the phone, elated and encouraged. Within days I connected with other similar-minded folks, and we formed a group called Concerned Citizens of Los Angeles. Our immediate mission was to go before the city council and be a voice of reason in favor of keeping the intelligence unit. At the same time, we would mobilize other citizens who felt the same way. A press conference held at the Los Angeles Press Club drew not only a large group that supported preventive law enforcement but also widespread attention from the local media. The tide was beginning to turn. Over the next months, we lobbied, wrote articles for papers, and appeared on news and talk shows.

A personal high point was when I was asked to debate leaders of the ACLU at one of its forums. I felt like Daniel heading into the lions' den or perhaps Elijah going *mano a mano* against the prophets of Baal. Still, just as God was with them, he was with me. My introduction was greeted with a smattering of applause and more than a few cold stares. As I surveyed the conference room, the faces looking back at me seemed to say, "Let's hear what you've got . . . fascist." I proceeded to present the facts in an unemotional manner. The membership listened with growing interest, then amazement, then concern. By the time I was finished, the majority offered its overwhelming support. Long before Fox News, I reported and let the people decide. On this occasion, the ACLU membership did not disappoint me, though its leadership wasn't too happy about the results of my presentation.

It is a truth that when we Americans are presented with facts we will usually respond the right way. I had started in motion what would eventually become thousands of people letting their voices be heard. And when the dust settled, we still had the intelligence-gathering unit in Los Angeles. This, I am convinced, is one of the reasons we had a safe Olympics in 1984.

Though we won the battle, the war was still raging. Those who wanted to see our way of life changed would be back another day. The biggest problem was—and still is—keeping Americans interested and active when everything seems to be going well. Sadly, as we'll see in later chapters, we were unable to stop the dismantling of our intelligence capability at the federal level as we had locally. On a clear September morning in 2001, our national disinterest would catch up to us with a deadly vengeance.

The information I received from my government friend Earl focused me on the job ahead. I had to build in each country the ability to gather information about terrorists and what they were planning. I started making a to-do list; topping the column was the enlistment of friends around the world in law enforcement. I arranged to be at my office at five o'clock the next morning to start dialing different time zones. There was no time to lose.

Naked and Exposed below the Border

FIVE A.M. WAS EARLY to be at the office, even for me. Not that I was any stranger to odd hours. In those days, I was still spending a lot of time on cases, particularly the undercover operations in which I teamed with local law enforcement for takedowns. Most of our busts were at night, so I'd wind up sleeping on the office couch, too tired to drive the thirty miles to my quiet, suburban home in the San Fernando Valley. But on this morning I was up with the fishermen, casting my communication lines to Paris, London, and Bonn to troll for whatever assistance I could find for building an international intelligence operation. With each call to my friends and contacts in these cities, I laid out what I was trying to do. Each response was the same: "How can I help?" Encouraged by their interest and input, I had a firm game plan worked out by the time my early-morning round of calls ended. Heeding the Lord's direction to Habbakuk to "write down this vision" (Hab. 2:2), I immediately poured my thoughts onto paper, preparing a detailed overview of my plan for each of the agents. This was the genesis of the International Intelligence Unit, and these initial contacts became my first station chiefs.

At about 9:00 a.m., George Otis called from Israel. He was in a panic. He said he had to pay for work being done, and we didn't have the money. "I've written checks High Adventure can't cover," he said. "Can you help in any way? Do you know anyone who could give fifty thousand dollars to the ministry—now?" Fifty grand is a whole different game from spotting someone a twenty. Still, as we talked, the name of a good friend came to mind: Bert Boeckmann. In addition to owning the leading Ford dealership in the country, Bert was a man of prayer and generosity toward worthy causes. (Then again, perhaps it's because he's a man of prayer and generosity that he has the leading Ford dealership in the country.) I told George I'd call Bert and find out if he was able to help. George stressed the urgency of our situation. "They don't look with favor on people who bounce checks over here." I placed a call to Bert's office and was able to get through—the day's first small miracle. I told him about the station, the situation in Lebanon and Israel, and what we were trying to do. "Bert, we're in a bind," I said. "We need fifty thousand dollars, and we need it really soon." Bert asked some questions about the schedule for building the station and then said, "Come by later today, and I'll have a check for fifty thousand dollars waiting for you." Wow, this was going to make George's day! "Get George on the phone!" I yelled to my assistant. The call went through, I gave him the news, and everyone could hear George's "Hallelujah!" all the way from the Holy Land. This was the first miracle of scores we'd see in the coming nine months as Voice of Hope came to life. Incidentally, since contributing to the Israeli-Lebanese effort, Bert's business has expanded and prospered dramatically. I hear echoes of God telling the Jews, "Those who bless you will be blessed."

And then, there's also the flip side: "Those who curse you will be cursed."

As I devoured every piece of information I could find on terrorism, the names of the groups that cursed Israel and all freedom-loving people filled my days and even invaded my dreams: PLO, Hamas, Popular Front for the Liberation of Palestine (PFLP), Hezbollah, Red Army Faction, ETA, and Action Directe. The more I learned about their evil the more my passion grew to fight them with everything I had. Soon this passion consumed the very direction of my life. As word spread that I was knowledgeable about terrorism, my phone begin to ring with speaking requests from clubs and government organizations in the Los Angeles area. Before I knew it, I was highly ranked on a number of speakers bureaus and my schedule got very intense. Ten to twelve times a week I was out lecturing on the subject of terrorism, sharing the facts about what was going on in the world and what was being planned for America. I found that most Americans responded much as I had when informed about the danger to our freedom. They offered to help. "Tell me what you want me to do," they'd say. At the same time, I was meeting with politicians and friends in the police department about the dangers Los Angeles was facing with the upcoming Olympics.

It was after one of these meetings that I received a call from someone identifying himself as a captain at the Los Angeles Police Department. He said he had been in the old intelligence unit at LAPD and had an interest in intelligence and counterterrorism. He said he had been given my name by my government friend Earl who said I was well versed on Middle Eastern terrorism. I asked this man—I'll call him Alex—to give me his number and I would call him back. After I hung up, I called Earl. "Do you know Captain Alex?" "Yeah," said Earl, "I gave him your number. I met him when he was with the intelligence unit at LAPD and thought he'd be a good contact for you." I called Alex back, told him I had checked him out and that he looked OK. "No problem," he laughed. "I expected you to." Once a detective, always a detective.

Alex revealed the primary reason for his call: "I have a family member going over to Israel for a few months, and I'm concerned about travel safety." I provided him an overview and suggested we get together so I could fill in the details. He brought up the Olympics and some of the statements I had made in the press about the danger of terrorists targeting this high-profile international event. Alex was going to be part of the LAPD's Olympic planning team and was interested in any insight I might offer. He went on to say he was interested in Mexico and had a great concern about the ability of terrorists to enter the United States from our southern border. (Remember, this conversation took place more than twenty years ago.) Alex offered to get me intelligence on developments in Baja California that pointed to Middle Eastern terrorist activity within easy reach of our border. The international spread of Middle Eastern terror groups suddenly became more than just a theory. If Alex was right, the enemy was camped on our southern border, quietly building its network while we were busy assuming we were secure in our safe, peaceful environment. It was the late '70s, and even then I had a sickening feeling that the question of terrorism striking America was not *if* but *when*. Terrorists were at our back door and it was unlocked; disco music was blasting so loudly in our ears we couldn't hear anybody enter.

The following day, I arranged a get-acquainted meeting with Alex so we could swap information. Normally, officers in public law enforcement couldn't share data with someone in the private sector, but in the intelligence business there were legal ways to work with public officers. Certainly, since 9/11 the government has opened up even more, realizing that the only way we will win this war against the terrorists is if the public and private security sectors work together and share information. The left hand has to know what the right is doing, or they both risk being chopped off.

Alex and I found we had many things in common, such as a love for Mexico and Europe and the desire to travel. He gave me a quick briefing on the PLO operation in Baja California and about all the money that was being funneled from there to the Middle East. Our government's focus was on illegal immigration and drug smuggling; our officials were very naive about terrorists on our southern border and were only starting to see the hand-prints of terrorism in the drug trade. There were two motives behind the drug-terror marriage: to raise money to support terror operations and infrastructure and to destroy the fabric of our society with drugs. The drug cartels were starting with our inner cities, understanding that we had thousands of young people living there who had little hope and no apparent way out of the poverty they had been born into. Drug cartels and terror groups understood that by offering pockets full of money they could contribute to the decline of our society, using our own people. They didn't need an army to invade the shores of America, only people already here who had been left out of the American dream.

What did we expect? The evidence was plentiful in broken-down, impoverished third world countries: When someone came along with a helping hand, even though the hand was evil, the people would follow. The (often) right-wing government would be overthrown, and the people would find themselves not free but under the brutal heels of leftists worse than the governments they had overthrown. Our nation was ripe for this sort of outbreak if we didn't wake up and get serious about solving the problems of our society. Handing out welfare wasn't the answer; we'd tried that for years and only succeeded in creating a subculture that made people dependent on a handout rather than a hand up. We gave them incentives to avoid work and disdain two-parent homes. Another direct consequence I witnessed in my private investigation business was the rise of workplace crime: I saw the dollars lost to employee theft and other malfeasance grow from tens of millions to billions each year.

It may sound odd to link domestic social problems to international terrorism, but I couldn't escape the connection. Terrorists—like the devil—seek to exploit weaknesses: in our vigilance, in our society, in ourselves. So, as I was speaking across the city, exposing the dangers of terrorism, I found myself also addressing this breakdown in the fabric of society. "If we want to see our streets become safer and our communities become places where our children can play without danger, we must address this problem at the root cause," I told them. "More police on the streets isn't the answer, because if you have citizens who don't respect other people or their property, having a cop on every street corner won't stop the violence." The fact is we can't replace the Golden Rule with "If it feels good, do it" and not expect long-term, negative consequences for our national security.

Over and over, I was asked how we could reverse this downward spiral. I responded that we must start at the kindergarten level and teach kids the very ethics that most of you reading this book already have—and which most in the media and liberal academics disdain. At the same time, we need to have swift, sure enforcement of our laws and quick punishment of those convicted—not years of maneuvering or evading justice by means of technicalities.

As Alex and I discussed in our first meeting, it's very difficult to turn a nation around. The process takes years, but it has to start somewhere. Just think how long the terrorists waited and planned before 9/11. Radical Islamists were dreaming of this day back in the '70s. They developed a long-term plan and didn't let anything or anyone deter them from their goals. Yes, they had setbacks, but they didn't let the defeats destroy them. They learned from their mistakes and in most cases didn't make them again. As I talked to Alex, I wondered: Would our country listen? Would we Americans learn from the mistakes of Europe? We had won a skirmish in Los Angeles with the successful fight to keep the LAPD's intelligence unit, but that was just the tip of the iceberg. *What about other cities?* I wondered, especially with our intelligence-gathering capability under attack at the federal level.

I was planning a trip to Europe to meet with my station chiefs, but Alex suggested I first visit Mexico, to meet some of the law enforcement and political leaders and see firsthand what was going on there. Alex was involved with Hands Across the Border, which helped police officers in Mexico by supplying them with medical care, equipment, and training. He was going down the next week and invited me to tag along. I quickly agreed; I loved visiting Mexico. The people were warm and friendly, the music infectious, and the sunsets on the beaches of Baja California amazing.

The Mexican Connection

The following Wednesday morning we were driving through border control and into Mexico. Crossing the border always made me think of entering another world. After being waved straight through the checkpoint, we pulled to the right where some police cars were parked. When we got out, we were mobbed like long-lost relatives by a host of police officials. Capt. Jose Campo embraced me as only the Mexicans can, and an instant bond developed between us. This warm, sincere man would become my guide and protector through many years of travel and adventure in Mexico.

We soon joined a gathering of a hundred brother officers from Baja at the police academy in Tijuana. Admittedly, the police in Mexico have had their share of bad apples, and unfortunately the

American press and Hollywood seem to pick up only on the dishonest officers, overlooking the many good guys. Over the past twenty years, I've met, worked with, and often come to treasure and love many good police officials south of the border. They deserve our respect and support.

At this first meeting, I developed many contacts for gathering intelligence on the terrorists in the Baja region. I discovered that PLO sympathizers had settled there, assuming lives amid the Mexican population and quickly going about their business of supporting the PLO. They were able to freely come and go from Mexico to the United States, using these trips to gather important intelligence that they transmitted to the Middle East. I also was told about other sympathizers: Mexican citizens who were funneling money back to the PLO treasury. These, for the most part, were anti-American and anti-Jewish, and willing to do anything that might hurt the United States or Israel. At that time, the PRI political party was still in power in Baja and had a measure of control on the criminal activity in the area. This all changed later as the opposition came to power in the state. The region became heavily infiltrated by the drug cartels, bringing lawlessness to the state, an area very crucial to the security of the United States.

I met the deputy chief of the Tijuana police. I'll call him Raul. Raul and I hit it off instantly. His background was in intelligence and medicine. A few minutes of conversation was all it took to see that he was well educated, thoughtful, and had a heart for honest, professional law enforcement. The Mexican government, very keen on keeping Baja a friendly place for tourists to visit, had sent Raul to root out corruption within the ranks of the department. I shared with him my vision of exposing the myth that Middle Eastern terrorism was about a Palestinian homeland; I told him of my belief that the terrorists' real purpose was to change the world into a radical Islamic society. Raul immediately offered to help, promising to give me information on what was going on in Baja. He also suggested I meet the mayor of Tijuana and the governor of Baja California. I quickly agreed.

Raul began telling me about local drug operations and the evidence he had collected indicating terrorist groups had begun working with—and in some cases, directing—the flow of drugs into the United States. He told of large movements of arms, including AK-47s, into the streets of southern California. Mexican intelligence had seen the handprints of the terrorists and the Soviet Union in these smuggling operations, a conclusion that fit the information I had gleaned in Lebanon.

The next day Raul called my office to say he had set up a meeting with the mayor and governor on the following Saturday. We'd be going to Rosetta Beach and then to Porto Nuevo to meet the governor. On the appointed day, I found myself sitting in the best seaside restaurant in the small town of Porto Nuevo, a guest of the state of Baja California. I began to get to know the governor, to learn what he was facing, and to learn his goals for his term in office. His primary objectives were to fight crime and reduce the drug cartels' influence on the region. We spoke together of "narco-terrorism" long before it became a familiar term. He saw the dangers in the drug cartels' alliance with terrorist groups and arms smugglers who saw the United States as their biggest market. He said his officers had to become the force standing between this evil and its march northward. Another concern was that rising crime and violence in Baja would negatively affect the thousands of tourists coming to the area each year. We developed a battle plan during this first meeting, committing ourselves to working together to fight against the terrorism and darkness seeking to destroy both our countries.

I started to realize how blessed I was to have found favor with these leaders. But I was also beginning to feel the weight of the great responsibility I was taking on; our common enemies would stop at nothing to eliminate those that got in their way. On the way back to the hotel, Raul and I talked about the future, our fears, and how we could work together. These conversations would continue for twenty years, as Raul became my close friend, business partner, and protector in Mexico.

I had a sort of extracurricular experience on that trip that I want to relate—at the risk of a little bit of personal embarrassment—that perfectly captures the image of the illicit activity on our southern border and its long-term implications for our national security. Raul and I, along with my wife at the time, were staying at the Rosetta Beach Hotel, a renowned hangout for Hollywood stars in the '30s and '40s. I was in a luxurious two-level suite and, after showering upstairs (and assuming my wife was the only other person in the suite), I got the notion of descending the stairs in what the Victorians used to call "a state of nature." Not to give away too many more details, let's just say I embellished my entrance with a few dance steps. Unknown to me, however, some of our other traveling companions were downstairs. Not only were they downstairs, but they captured my act on video. Needless to say, I still haven't lived down the humiliation of that miscalculation.

Still, my mortifying experience is a perfect metaphor for the situation we were facing—and still face today—on our southern border. The truth is we all are exposed right now. Unprepared and unsuspecting, America is coming down the stairs, dancing around with no idea what's waiting for us below. We are naked and vulnerable and being watched.

As we left Mexico, it hit me with the force of a Magnum bullet why this region would be a breeding ground for terrorists. The people we passed were living in such poverty, and, worse, they had little hope. When people don't have hope they will follow anyone or anything that offers it. "You have no hope on earth," the terrorist says, "but we'll promise you paradise in the next world. And all it costs is this life you already despise."

I knew we not only had to awaken the citizens of America to the danger posed by the Middle Eastern terrorists but also to the powder keg on our southern border.

My own education was only beginning. I was beginning to see the results of a terrorist's mind-set but still didn't know what caused it. I had an inkling of where terrorism was headed but not where it started. Was terrorism a product of the Middle East? Or was terrorism born of something deeper, broader, more ancient, and ingrained?

My journey toward the truth continued.

Origins of Terrorism

WHERE DID TERRORISM BEGIN? Did the PLO just think it up, or is there a trail we can follow into the past? Certainly, in one sense at least, we can follow the trail to the time just after Adam and Eve left the Garden of Eden. Violence and war have been with us since man's fall; God's intentions for a peaceful, personal relationship with those created in his image was rudely altered that day in Eden when man chose to listen to a seductive voice promising a better life than the one God envisioned. With the oldest son of Adam came the first murder, introducing another evil to a creation conceived and intended for purity. As we then explore the growth and unfolding of humanity, we see a sad record of how evil and violence emerge when we allow thoughts of power, wealth, sex, and pride to convince us we have a right to please ourselves.

Many scoffed when President Bush said after 9/11 that the war on terror is a fight between good and evil. However, as we trace the history of man, we find some who are cruel and ruthless and do unbelievable things, even to their own families and countrymen. Others are fair, kind, and endeavor to keep the best interests of their countrymen at heart. When we look at the two groups and follow their rise to power, we find that the evil groups surround themselves with advisers who urge leaders to be cruel, to keep the people in bondage, and, often, to worship false gods. On the other hand, those leaders who rule with fairness and concern for the people have advisers who counsel them to follow God's laws and to treat people with fairness. Regardless of religious belief, if any of us were given a choice, who wouldn't choose to live under the rule of those who rule with fairness and concern for their citizens? Surely we'd choose those who cherish life over those who deal in death. We'd choose the way of God, the way of blessing, over the way of curses. Long before Dr. Phil, the Lord was posing a challenge to people and governments: You can follow a path of life and abundance or one of decay and diminished returns. You can act for good, or you can act for evil.

It is unfashionable in our postmodern society to speak of good and evil. It's considered a quaint, superstitious concept for the simpleminded. Even when a president of the United States uses such language, there are those who dismiss it as naive or as a failure to appreciate the differences in cultures. However, if good and evil are subjective, depending only on one's point of view, then I should have no complaint when a gun is put to my head, when a child is molested, when 6 million people are gassed, or when a group of men decide to fly planeloads of people into crowded buildings. Denying the existence of good and evil is a way to refuse responsibility for our own wrongs or to excuse the wrongs of others. We'll have more to say on the spiritual element of the terror fight later, but for the moment we'll leave it with the fact that evil exists, and any reasonable person can quickly see that evil always works to stamp out good.

The cycle of evil and violence began with the Fall, and in the Bible we can read of its ebb and flow, as leaders of God's people either obeyed or failed to obey the Creator's intentions for humanity. But the pattern is hardly limited to the Holy Land. Violence has survived through the ages; and the more advanced our civilization has become, the more efficient our violence has become as well. We have found new ways to be cruel and inflict more pain on a greater number of people. We have seen Nietzsche's maxim "Kill one, scare a thousand" become the modus operandi of the modern terrorist.

Political Ends, Violent Means

Terrorism is a "systematic use of fear to further a political, social, or religious agenda." It comes from the French Revolution.

In the summer of 1793, the Committee of Public Safety controlled France's government. This small group of politicians ruled through systematic political repression, to put it euphemistically. Those subject to the campaign of intimidation and violence had another name for it: the Reign of Terror. The committee claimed to be acting on behalf of the people and the cause of democracy. How beheading people helped them is anyone's guess.

The orchestrator of this dark regime was Maximilien Robespierre who, in his thankfully brief thirty-six years, brought the word *terrorism* to life, using violence in a way the world had not seen before. During his short time in power, he and his Jacobin Club executed twelve thousand people deemed enemies of the revolution: many on mere suspicion, many more on fabricated charges. During one forty-seven-day period, 1,376 people met "Madame Guillotine," many of them the brightest, most promising minds of France. What a perversion of the original French vision, as journalist and revolution leader Camille Desmoulins wrote his wife Lucile Duplessis from prison: "I have dreamed of a republic which every one adored. I cannot believe that these people could be so wild and so unjust." Desmoulins would soon be executed, as would his wife.

Since the Jacobins ruled France, we technically wouldn't call them terrorists by a modern definition. They were authoritarian dictators, more Saddam than Osama. Still, the Jacobins' vision of violent purges in the name of utopia provided a model for terrorists to come. Where do such evil men come from? Why are they so quick to use murder and torture to get their way? Robespierre's story suggests some answers.

Robespierre was born May 6, 1758, in Arras, France, where his father practiced law. When Robespierre was nine, his mother died in childbirth. Shortly thereafter, his father suffered a breakdown, leaving him unable to care for his four children (reminiscent of Saddam and, for that matter, Yasser Arafat). After being passed around to a variety of relatives, Robespierre landed at a college in Arras before going to study law in Paris. He was admitted to the bar in 1781 and, like his father before him, successfully practiced law in his hometown of Arras. Active in literary and philosophical circles, Robespierre became devoted to the social theories of the French philosopher Jean Jacques Rousseau. In fact, he became fanatic, maintaining radical views Rousseau himself had abandoned. He gradually—perhaps inevitably—gravitated toward politics. Before his thirty-first birthday, Robespierre was elected as a third-estate deputy of Artois to the Estate-General at Versailles; that is, he was elected from among the common people rather than from the aristocracy. Robespierre's oratorical skills soon drew as many as thirty of his fellow deputies into a similar fanatical appreciation for Rousseau, particularly his "Social Contract." These deputies then formed a Society of the Friends of the Constitution, or the Jacobin Club as it was also called, with the aim of keeping the revolution "pure" by whatever means necessary. And so was born the Reign of Terror.

It's interesting, given the current world crisis, to note that the French Revolution was also sparked in part by religion. In France, the revolutionists believed it was necessary to root out the established religious institutions and beliefs as well as the age-old conflict between the classes. If innocent people had to die, so be it. Similarly—and to an even greater degree—bin Laden and others like him believe they have to change the established religious roots of a country to their own liking and that terror is appropriate to achieve that goal. If innocent people have to die, then it is Allah's will. They also have followed the French model in another manner: As the French revolutionists established footholds in different parts of France, today's terrorist organizations have established terror cells all over the world, set to act at the ordered time to support the cause. But terrorists should take note of the fate of the perpetrators of the Reign of Terror. Historically, such regimes tend to be relatively short-lived. Those who rule with extreme cruelty tend to bring about their own demise. Unlike the American Revolution, the French Revolution was a failure. Less than thirty years after the "Declaration of the Rights of Man" was penned and Marie Antoinette lost her head, a monarch again sat on the French throne. Even more telling is this fact: Since 1793, France has scrapped ten constitutions and enacted eleven new ones, while the United States still uses the same constitution formulated in the wake of our war for independence.

If modern terrorism was born in France, it grew up in Russia. The late 1800s saw the spread of Marxism. Marxists held that violence was a justifiable means for promoting their cause. During the Russian Revolution, an organization called Land and Freedom faced an internal split over whether propaganda or terror would best suit its purpose. And what happened? We find this account from records and research of the observations from those who lived during this time. The accounts sound eerily current: "Women who were once teaching children turned instead to the blowing up of trains.

Men who sought success in the business world and the wealth that went with it stabbed other human beings until their hands as well as their daggers were red with blood. Young people who had a passion to help the poor instead took to disguise and traveled from city to city, planting bombs in suitcases and bags."

Long before suicide bombers left behind videos trumpeting their murderous "martyrdom," these Russian revolutionaries published tales of their heroism and martyrdom as if their methods had been vindicated. Actually, the czar's assassination ultimately resulted in the destruction of their comrades and their cause. Who were these people? What did they seek? Why did they decide on violence? It's clear from historical accounts that they did not turn to violence only when peaceful means failed. Instead, their writings display pride in their local accomplishments; they believed they were winning friends and gaining support and felt themselves to be operating within the framework and ideology of the new Land and Freedom program.

Terror was intended as a limited tool to win over the peasantry. But during the winter of 1878–79, violence bred violence, and the mystique of terrorism became ever more fascinating to the Russian revolutionaries. As police and other authorities took harsh measures in response, the terrorists called for more and more dramatic revenge against the government. It was the proposed assassination of Alexander II that brought the long-simmering division between terrorists and propagandists to a head. Those who wished to fight with ideas lost out to those who chose to fight with fear. The end result was millions of dead during the Soviet era and ultimately—as is the fate of all who seek to rule by terror—failure. Communism collapsed in Russia. Freedom won the Cold War.

Exporting Violence

The next spike in the use of violence and terrorism came with the current struggle in the Middle East. The Arab enemies of Israel took up the tool of terrorism when it became apparent they couldn't stop the creation of the Jewish state. Rejecting the idea of nations coexisting in peace, campaigns of terror and war were launched against Israel from the very day the UN approved the creation of modern Israel. The leaders of these Middle Eastern terror groups studied the tactics of the French revolutionists and patterned their violent approach after the Reign of Terror. They were also given support from the Soviet Union, which had long experience in the use of terror as a means of control.

The violence spread out of the Middle East into Europe and was in full force across the continent in the 1970s and '80s. The goal was to bring down the established governments and replace them with a socialist society pledged to help the poor and the working classes. John Lennon sang wistfully of a "brotherhood of man," but where socialism came in on the wings of the terror campaigns, it brought a living hell. For example, France in the '70s and '80s followed a policy of appeasement. One could almost say the French were more accommodating to international terrorists than they were to American tourists. For example, on a single day of amnesty in 1978, the French government released hundreds of imprisoned terrorist suspects. France was opening its borders and allowing the terrorists to live and operate on their soil with the under-standing that the bad guys wouldn't do their dirty work on French soil. This worked for awhile, but in the '80s world opinion began shifting and France came under pressure to stop providing the terrorists a haven. Still, the French resisted, until the policy blew up in their faces.

On one frightful day in 1986, twelve bombs exploded across Paris, bombs set by some of those same terrorists France had released. This straw broke the camel's back for the French people. They told their government, "Enough! The appeasement must stop!" This was the beginning of the end for the terrorists in France, as the government heeded the call of the people, set up aggressive counterterrorist units, and set out to destroy the terrorist cells. Unfortunately, as indicated by France's friendship with Saddam Hussein, its lax attitudes toward acts of violence against Jews, and its welcome to radical Islamists, the French again appear to be falling into the deadly trap of appeasement, to their own peril.

If we track the growth of violence in a society, twenty-five-year cycles appear to emerge. One of these cycles started in the mid-1960s and tapered off in the early '90s (which contributed to the complacency that left us vulnerable on 9/11). The real end to that cycle came with the fall of the Iron Curtain and the demise of the Soviet Union, which had continued to be a major supporter and integral part of the Middle Eastern terrorist expansion in Europe. With the Soviet Union tossed on the trash heap of history, the pipeline of support dried up and we saw a dramatic decline in world terrorism.

The sense we were in a safer world swept over Europe and the United States like a potent narcotic. But every high has a crash waiting in the wings. With the loss of support from the Soviets, terror groups looking to destabilize the West went looking for another champion. Who would rise up and take on the Western Satan and bring about the mother of all wars? They needed someone committed to a holy war, someone who had mobility, access to funds, logistics, and the ability to bring together the terror cells that had been developed by Iran and radical Islamists from across the globe. An unlikely candidate rose to the top: a billionaire's son from Saudi Arabia who was versed in business, who hated the West, and who wanted to bring a radical Islamic government to the world. His name was Osama bin Laden.

A Man on a Mission

He had demonstrated his commitment in Afghanistan against the Soviets, earning the loyalty of the international *mujahideen* who fought there. He could form al-Qaeda and take up where the Iranians left off. It was just about ten years from the birth of al-Qaeda to September 11, 2001. That's a stunning amount of organizational growth, but not if part of the plan includes incorporating smaller groups already in existence. Even terror groups enjoyed merger mania in the '90s. Unfortunately, 9/11 was not the end. Our enemy continues to grow and expand. The new twenty-five-year cycle of violence got under way in the late '90s, and we aren't even at the halfway point. With the weapons available to the terrorists now, what we have in store for us will make the '70s and '80s look like child's play, if we don't stop them first.

What has our brief walk on the trail of terrorism shown us? From the French to the Communists to the Islamists, the face of terrorism hasn't changed since it was first used as a means to take over a country. Leon Trotsky, one of the fathers of the Bolshevik revolution, wrote a major work titled *In Defense of Terrorism*. Trotsky made a virtue of necessity and argued that terror was necessary not only for the protection of the Soviet regime but for the advance of socialism. In a famous piece of rhetoric, he declared, "Who aims at the end cannot reject the means," and "If human life is sacred or inviolable, we must deny ourselves not only the use of terror, not only war, but the Revolution itself." But what made Trotsky's terrorism better than the violence of the existing government? The goal, he said: socialism. "Terror is helpless," he declared, "if employed by reaction against a histor-ically rising class . . ." but terror *is* effective, he suggested, when used in the service of historical development. "We have sup-pressed those against us and they have disappeared," Trotsky said, and that was good enough for him, at least until those same guns took aim at him.

Today we are faced with the radical Islamic terrorist who insists his desired end—Islamic rule—justifies any means. He insists violence is the path laid out by Allah for those who don't follow his lead. This view begs so many questions: If terrorists hold the solution to the world's problems, why aren't we running to join them? Why are the countries that do embrace their views such dismal failures? More importantly, if their beliefs are so great and are correct, why should they have to force us to join their camp or be killed? It takes an incredible lack of faith to blow up the marketplace of ideas rather than offer your own. How weak is their god that his message can be delivered only by murder?

Yet, today they spread out across the world, working to con-vince Muslim countries and Muslim minorities abroad that their way offers a better, more righteous life. Beware of this kind of talk. The words may have changed from the French and Russian revolutions, but the tune is the same. Those who listened and were seduced suffered great violence and loss of life.

We must unmask the terrorist and show him to the world as the evil destroyer of freedom that he is.

And remember, as we noted at the top of this chapter, we must look also within ourselves. What causes this cycle of violence to be used over and over by new generations who find new and more advanced ways to be cruel to their fellow man? I think we have to agree that within each one of us is the potential for evil. It comes out when we put ourselves, our viewpoints, our wants, and our desires before everyone and everything else. Our pride and lust for power drive us to suppress our consciences and respect for the rights of others. Then we, like the cruel leaders throughout history, gather around us "yes people" who feed our egos, building for us a comfort zone that shields us from hearing truth and justice or acting with love and compassion. This holds true from Robespierre to Lenin, from Yasser Arafat to Osama bin Laden, from the CEO of Enron to the face we see in the mirror.

How can we explain this universal potential for evil that lurks in the heart of every human being regardless of race, religion, or culture? To find this answer—and to come face-to-face with the source of all hatred, all violence, all terror—we must enter the next chapter of our quest.

The Spiritual Origin of Violence

IT WAS LATE 1978, and the question was coming from terror-ist experts and average citizens: "Where did all this violence and hatred come from?" We've already attempted a brief history of modern terrorism, but as I began to investigate the facts, I came to the conclusion that the answer lay further back. But how far?

Like many people, I had always thought of the struggles in the Middle East as originating with the events shown in Genesis 6, when Jacob stole Esau's birthright; the division that developed from that deception brought about two nations that have warred ever since. Or, we might go back a generation earlier to Isaac and Ishmael. In fact, we've even traced terrorism to man's earliest days, citing violence as part of the human condition since the Fall. But have we really reached the essence of terrorism? Are we look-ing at the original *cause* or merely the *effect*?

Look again at the first murder recorded in the Bible: Cain murdering his brother Abel. We could draw the conclusion that this was the beginning of violence. But was it? What force drove Cain to murder? We can't blame the influence of TV, a troubled childhood, or the abundance of weapons on the street. We can't even blame a primal animal survival instinct; Abel wasn't acting in any threatening way toward his brother. So what force drove Cain to murder? What *cause* leads to the *effect* of violence?

I submit that the apostle Paul was right when he said in Ephesians 6:12 our battle is not with flesh and blood but principalities and powers—unseen spiritual forces. I submit that the start of terrorism is found beyond the Garden, in the very depths of heaven itself with the birth of evil.

The point of this discussion is not to get you into a church; it's to show you the heart of terrorism and the root of all other evil. Even if you don't believe the literal truth of the Bible, I ask that you follow along and find the allegorical truth about terrorism that the biblical story holds.

A Battle in Heaven

As an investigator, I must be clear with a client about what I know and what I don't know. In this case, we don't know a lot about heaven; we have no idea, for instance, how long heaven existed before the events under consideration. We have no idea how God, who exists outside time, views or accounts for time. The poetic language of the Bible reveals these things as best we can understand them, but even this description pales when compared to the reality. We do know that heaven is a place of great joy and peace; God is in control and he is perfect, just, righteous, holy, loving, forgiving, and has great patience with his children.

Apparently this wasn't good enough for some of the angels living in this paradise. In fact, the one who is called the most beautiful of all the angels decided he could do better than God and managed to persuade one-third of the angels to follow him (Rev. 8:12; 12:7).

Satan's pride led to the first battle between good and evil; the first act of terrorism happened in God's own realm. When we look at the rebellion in heaven, we must conclude that acts of terrorism are spiritual, for the first act of terrorism was concocted to turn the good of heaven into the evil that Lucifer desired to put in its place.

The Battle Comes to Earth

Lucifer's plot failed. He was defeated by the God of heaven, cast out, and exiled to an existence of torment but with the freedom to try to seduce others to follow him. We next pick up Lucifer's trail in the Garden of Eden as the serpent or tempter. The battle between good and evil had moved down to earth.

The same Lucifer whose cunning, beauty, and mastery of words made him able to deceive a third of the angels in heaven took aim at Eve and Adam. Though they knew the presence of God in a way no human has enjoyed since, they listened to the words of the deceiver and chose their own desires above God's will for them. Sadly, all of us have made the same poor choice. Such are the consequences of listening to the voice of evil.

I must admit I have many questions about the history of the world, and I know that many of them won't be answered until I am in the presence of God and "all will become clear." I sometimes wonder, for example, why God didn't destroy Satan when he defeated him in heaven. There are many instances in the Old Testament when God commanded the destruction of his enemies, but for some reason he allowed Satan to continue.

I think the answer has something to do with God's love and ultimate desire for his children. He wants us to come to him freely, of our own desire; he doesn't want to force us or compel us or give us an existence in which we have only one possible choice.

We must state clearly that God doesn't make mistakes; but we also know he allows humans, who are made in his image, to make mistakes. It seems to me that God's gift of choice means nothing if it doesn't include the option to choose badly—to turn our backs on him, even. Free will is meaningless if there are no good or bad consequences. Risk ceases to exist; reward loses all value. Life is drained of any preciousness, and we have no capacity for growth. (How good would a skier become if falling down or smashing into trees didn't hurt? For that matter, would there be any thrill or excitement?)

It is for our fullness and fulfillment that we have free will, even when we choose darkness over light. But the very nature of God doesn't rest with our bad choices. He tries to bring us back to his care and protection by loving us into making the choice to come back freely to him. Unlike Satan, however, he doesn't use threats, coercion, or lies.

The Battle Continues

Satan tried to defeat God head-on but failed. Now he's trying to defeat God by perverting his special creation: humanity—you and me. Specifically, his fallback strategy is to separate us from God. The book of Job describes how he is busy accusing us before God. I'm sure my sins alone would give him plenty to talk about.

Satan is not only an accuser; as we've seen he's also a deceiver. At the end of the day, because he truly has no power over us that we don't give him, he has to use the tool of deception. Take poor Job, for example; he thought God was punishing him. He was deceived into believing that the work of evil was an act of God. Doesn't that sound familiar? Aren't al-Qaeda members deceived into thinking their work of evil is actually an act of God?

Don't you be deceived: Man by man, woman by woman, Satan is diverting as many as he can from the kingdom of God to the kingdom of hell. The specific tactics change as the times change. He'll use love, money, power, politics—even religion. He puts his deception in the mouths of our enemies: "Follow our violent path and we will set you free."

And there are other deceptions carried out every day: Organizations claim to be moderate while funneling money to terrorists, then accuse those who call them to task of slandering all Muslims. Muslim students at religiously funded schools in the United States are taught that the United States is the enemy. American students at American-funded schools are taught that America deserves to be the enemy. The public is told that the war on terrorism should be directed only against al-Qaeda since it is supposedly solely responsible for 9/11. Each day, Muslim children are being taught that paradise awaits them across the blown-apart bodies of innocent strangers.

It is very apparent that there is an evil force at work on earth. The notion of some that Satan has already been locked in hell is demonstrably false. The scriptural record states that our accuser roams the earth looking for those he can accuse—or devour (1 Pet. 5:8). It doesn't take long, looking at the violence and evil in our society, to admit that the dragon of Revelation 12 is still breathing fire into man's flesh.

One of his most effective strategies, just as with Adam and Eve, is to convince us that because we want something we therefore deserve it. We'll go to great lengths, jump high hurdles, and take crazy chances just to have what we desire in our hearts, even if what we desire is really bad for us. Consider again the deception that came into the mind of Jacob's mother; she coached him to deceive Isaac into believing that Jacob was Esau so he could steal the birthright. Do you think that Satan's desire was simply for the theft of the birthright? I submit that he may have been thinking centuries down the road, to a time when this deception would inflame the world with such hatred that the fight would ultimately destroy God's creation. Be it al-Qaeda or Satan, our enemy is taking the long view.

So many times in a long-standing conflict, the original cause or motive has been pushed so far back no one even remembers the reason. Instead, both sides just keep the hate alive. Satan delights in using the part of our nature that can't forgive or admit we are wrong. How far this is from the nature of God: humble and forgiving. We listen to the voices around that encourage us to keep up the fight "for our rights."

The brainwashed young suicide bombers are obeying voices that fill them with phantom angers, with false injustices that stoke their passions, causing them to give their lives in a fight with an enemy that would just as soon be their friend. I'm picturing one particular suicide attack in Israel in 2003: Both the Palestinian bomber and Jewish victim were around twenty years old, both female, both beautiful, both smart, both loved and respected by their friends and colleagues. Pictured side by side, they looked as if they could be cousins, sorority sisters, or shopping buddies. But instead of planning careers and families together, they're both dead, victimized by a hatred neither had a hand in creating. The bomber was a pawn in the hands of men corrupted by evil thoughts woven into the very fabric of their minds by the most devious of all deceivers.

To me, the shattered bodies of these two women perfectly symbolize an undeniable truth: Evil is real. Evil is at work. Evil works to deceive. Evil deceives in order to destroy.

Even if you have never thought about God or been a part of any religion, I encourage you to explore the facts. If I'm wrong, what do you have to lose? But if I'm right—that terrorism at its most fundamental level is a spiritual battle in which the existence of our world is at stake—wouldn't your support be justified? I ask you to continue reading this book with an open mind, with a greater sensitivity to the spiritual nature of terrorism, even as we deal with the worldly workings of the modern terrorist.

We've taken a necessary detour into the history and sources of terrorism. Conducting background work is crucial to any good investigation. But at some point, we have to get back on the street, and the time has come to rejoin the chase for today's terrorists. In my case, the chase took me back to Lebanon.

Life and Death in Lebanon

KEEPING THE VOW I'd made in Lebanon, I continued my efforts to develop an international intelligence-gathering network. I started with Israel, then moved through Europe, recruiting agents in England, France, Germany, and Italy. I hired as the head of my international operation a retired intelligence operations captain from the Los Angeles Police Department. Raul was also instrumental in establishing our office in Tijuana, which soon covered the entire Latin American region. In 1980, I looked to the East; I met Li Fu Ki, who had set up an operation in Hong Kong after retiring as head of the Hong Kong police department's criminal investigation division. We became immediate friends, and he agreed to develop our stations across the Far East. Within a year I had visited Bangkok, Singapore, Taiwan, and the Philippines, positioning station chiefs in each locale.

As my network developed, one of my first international tasks was to help gather information in preparation for the 1984 Olympics to be hosted by Los Angeles. Part of that task included traveling to Europe with a group of American law enforcement personnel to study how the Europeans were battling terrorism and to absorb the lessons learned from the 1972 Olympic massacre in Munich.

During all this travel—particularly when reminded of what Palestinian terrorists had done in Munich, far from the Middle East—my focus kept returning to Lebanon. By the spring of 1982, I had been in and out of Lebanon many times; each visit brought a more frightening realization that we were dealing with an evil that ultimately could engulf the world. Israel was continuing to take losses from the missiles fired across the northern border from the high perch of Beufort Castle. I was beginning to pick up rumblings from my contacts there that Israel was considering going north and taking out the castle.

Although our Voice of Hope radio station in Lebanon had been on the air for three years, I had a very real concern for it and the TV station we also had built. The TV station's tower was farther north toward Beirut, perched across the top of Maroun er Ras. We wanted to be near the water because that would help increase our transmission range. The downside was it also increased our exposure and risk from the PLO. What if the Israelis pulled out of Lebanon? Where would that leave us? I knew the Israelis were close to the breaking point. Anger and frustration crept increasingly into the voices of my friends and contacts until, by May 1982, they were openly shouting to me and anyone who would listen: "The violence against the innocent must stop!"

Going Back

I was mulling the implications of any Israeli action when, as if by divine arrangement, my intercom announced, "George is on the line." George got right to the point. "Phil," he said, "I'm concerned about the station and the towers." He was rattling off words like a machine gun. "You need to go over and put more early-warning security devices around the station and towers. When can you leave?" When a spirit of urgency hits George, he charges like the Oakland Raiders special teams. He didn't even consider that I might not be able to drop everything and go . . . and he was right. I needed to keep the intelligence flowing from

Lebanon, and there was nothing like being on the ground there to ensure it. "I'll put together the equipment and let you know when I can leave," I told him. George wasn't satisfied with my sense of urgency: "We need to move *quickly.*" Hanging up the phone, a thought popped into my mind: *How am I going to get a bunch of security equipment through customs in Israel?* When I later mentioned this to George, his answer was as matter-of-fact as it was crazy: "You put it in your luggage and walk through." I knew Israeli airport security people weren't like their American counterparts at that time: They were very attentive, highly trained pros who didn't let people wander into their country— especially if they were carrying unidentified electronic equipment. "What if they stop me?" I said. "Look, Phil, if you get stopped, just tell them it's for the army." Easy for him to say, because he wouldn't be the one getting up close and personal with Israeli interrogation techniques.

Over the next few days, I gathered all the necessary equipment, fashioning a transistor-operated wireless system that would be easy to install and more importantly, show fewer bulges in my baggage for the Israelis to see. They'd mastered the art of profiling; they had people whose sole job was to observe someone walking off a plane and into the baggage area. These sharp-eyed professionals—behavioral experts, actually—knew what to look for, including nationality, dress, and subtle, telltale actions. Because I knew the profile, I was mentally running through all the things not to do and reminding myself that if the worst-case scenario happened and I was stopped, I could always call our military contact. I rechecked the equipment list as well as all the supplies I would need to install the system. There'd be no running to Radio Shack if I overlooked something. This was the time to practice what I preached to my troops: Check and recheck, and check again.

The plan was to set up a base unit in the radio studio so the station operator could summon the military if someone was spotted tampering with the towers. It wasn't until I was on the plane that I realized an obvious flaw in the plan: If a terrorist used a bomb or missile, my little early-warning devices would be like toys. Oh well, I wanted to go to Lebanon anyway.

The British Airways flight to Tel Aviv via London was fourteen hours, far too much time to think about that long walk through customs and what I'd do if stopped. A dozen scenarios played out in my imagination, each more troubling than the last. Isn't it interesting how we create problems in our minds before we really have them, even if we're experienced international private eyes who have faced the wrong end of weapons? I knew from the Bible that my fears would find me out, so I tried putting out of my mind the thought of being stopped. *Anyway,* I thought, *I'm the good guy.* I was helping the embattled Christians in southern Lebanon, which also helped Israel's situation. That sounded like a good line if I was checked and they realized I had enough electronic gear on me to stock a Circuit City.

Running the Gauntlet

When my plane touched down in Israel, I stowed my fear and let my training kick in. I was dressed as a tourist and looked American, which in this case was good. The only negative that might cause me to be stopped was lugging three large suitcases despite traveling alone. I pondered the situation. Maybe I could find a single girl and ask her to be my stand-in wife. Surveying the crowd, I decided that option didn't look promising. So as I waited for my bags, I tried to act touristy and not be impatient. When my bags came, I placed them on a cart, trying to make them look as small as possible. With a deep breath I started walking toward the exit where there were two lines: one for those with something to declare and another for those with nothing to declare. Casually, with jet-weary indifference, I headed for the line that would lead me directly to the terminal. I looked around and smiled at the customs agents off to the side but didn't hold their gaze more than a few seconds and kept walking. I also was praying. I was on God's mission and thought I could expect his favor. Of course, I was also expecting with each step to hear, "You there! Over here, so we can check your bags." Closer and closer I moved toward the exit and still no order to stop. "C'mon, just a little farther," I muttered to myself. Finally, I reached the exit, breaking through that magical barrier with an enormous sense of relief while resisting the urge to shout, "I made it!" A celebratory dance was clearly not in order. Nonetheless, I was in the terminal, I felt like a million dollars, and the pressure was off. *That was more stressful than having missiles fired at me in southern Lebanon,* I thought. Little did I know that within forty-eight hours I'd be completely redefining my concept of the word *stress.*

Motoring away from the airport in my rental car, I spotted a group of soldiers hitchhiking. I pulled over and discovered they were heading, like me, to the northern front. As is the custom, I stopped and picked up as many as my car would hold—three in all. This was no mere humanitarian gesture: It wouldn't hurt to have three heavily-armed soldiers on board in the event we should encounter terrorists on the way to the Lebanese border— a tip I'd gotten from one of my friends in the Israeli military.

Two hours later, I was dropping off the soldiers at the Metulla military base and heading for the Arrizme Hotel. I was ready for a long sleep. A quick recon indicated nothing appeared to have changed since my last visit. However, as I settled in for an early dinner at the hotel, I immediately sensed something was going on. The air seemed to crackle with expectation. Looking around the dining room, I noticed a lot of Westerners. Eavesdropping on some conversations, I learned that they were reporters, and they were anticipating some major military event. This was near the end of May 1982, and military action around the border had increased noticeably. I had not yet talked to Colonel Yourm or anyone from the Israeli military command but deduced the buzz might be related to Israel's decision to do something to stop the murderous shelling by the PLO. Because I already had my pass, I could have just driven across, but an inner voice said, *Be wise. Check with Yourm.*

After exchanging greetings and bringing each other up to date on our families, I let Yourm know I was on the ground and planning to head into Lebanon the next day. "Oh. The violence has increased over the last few months, Phil, and the high command in Tel Aviv is running out of patience. Troops are being massed on the northern border." And then, not very cryptically, he added, "In a short time we will stop the shelling."

He did not elaborate. He merely advised me to be very careful if I went into Lebanon. PLO activity had shifted farther south than in the past, and my destination would be well within the PLO circle of operation. I told him I estimated installing the security equipment would take a couple of days. "Be careful," he said, emphasizing the point by handing me an Uzi and extra clips. "You'll be on your own, and if you get into trouble, by the time backup gets to you, it'll be too late."

Sleep was difficult at first. With each exciting thought of the cutting-edge, world-changing mission I was on, there came a moment of sanity. "I have two children at home, and I want to see them grow up." When I did drift to sleep, it was in prayer: *God, protect me.*

I was up at 6:00 a.m. and soon was enjoying my morning coffee and the magnificent view of Mount Hermon. My reverie was

disturbed by an unusual swarm of early morning activity sur-
rounding the hotel, apparently from the vast media contingent
that had descended on Metulla. Later, as I drove toward the
Good Fence gate, I could feel the eyes of the international press
corps on me. No doubt, the reporters were asking, "How's *he*
getting into Lebanon?" I offered a cheerful wave and headed
through.

The radio studio was only two miles inside the border. When
I got to the studio, I let the station operator know I would be at
the towers and transmitters, installing the security equipment.
The transmitter building was close to the studio and out of sight
of Beufort Castle and the PLO missiles. I plopped down my tools
and supplies and set to work. It took about four hours to complete the installation and testing of the security system, ensuring
it would transmit to the studio. Because I'd brought my lunch, I
didn't have to go back to Metulla to eat. Devouring the goodies,
I drove to the towers, a short distance away, and began setting
up the early-warning devices around the tower base. This was all
the easy part. The real test would be when I went north toward
Beirut—and the roving PLO hit teams—to install the equipment
at the TV tower.

I wrapped up work at the radio towers and was back at the
Arrizme by 6:00 p.m., showering off the dust and dirt and thinking of delicious Middle Eastern cuisine. I was at the hotel café
only a few minutes before company arrived at my table, a producer working for one of the American news networks. He'd
seen me go across the border. "How'd you get a permit to get
across when we haven't been able to?" Soon, I had reporters and
producers from all three major U.S. networks (this was in the
days before CNN and Fox) at my table, trying to figure out how
they could get into Lebanon with my help. One offered a very
nice pile of cash if I would smuggle him through the border in the

trunk of my car. Others proposed all kinds of harebrained ideas that I quickly nixed. They were still tugging at my sleeves even as I left the table. When I recounted the offers with Colonel Yourm, he laughed and said, "I'm not surprised," adding, "We're not letting them through. We know that if the American press gets into Lebanon, they'll send biased reports, making us look bad, just like they do at the northern front." Israel was determined not to be burned this time.

I told Colonel Yourm that I'd still be going north to Maroun er Ras the next day. He gave me a worried look. "Make sure your radio is charged in case you need help." As I went back to the hotel, I was thoughtful and a little anxious. Believe it or not, the risk-taking, adventure-loving international private eye was having second thoughts about this trip north to the TV towers. In the forefront of my mind was the fact that my name and my address in the States were on a PLO hit list and had been broadcast over the PLO radio waves. Did they know I was here? How good was their intelligence on the Israeli side of the border? Did they have the ability to check on who was staying at the hotel? I had not registered under an assumed name. Going in without a cover was not an act of bravado or machismo; to be truthful, it hadn't entered my mind until that very moment that registering under my own name wasn't the smartest thing to do. Fortunately, I had a great trust that the God of Abraham, Isaac, and Jacob would watch over me and protect me the next day. Knowing his hand was on me and that I was here on a mission to help people in need, I drifted off to a peaceful night's sleep.

Baptism by Fire

BY 8:00 A.M. I was loading my car, carefully checking my weapon, and making sure I had the spare clips in the front seat. I love the quiet of the morning, but today's stillness was spoiled by the barking of the media hounds. Again, they scurried toward me, waving increasingly lucrative offers of payment to take them into Lebanon. "No, thank you!" I repeated, adding, "My permit is for one, and they check the car." I knew the soldiers would probably wave me through because they knew me and trusted me, but I wasn't telling that to the reporters. There wasn't any way I was going to break that trust, no matter how much money they offered. But I had to give the press boys an *E* for effort.

My first stop was at the radio station, to check the monitoring equipment and let the operator know I was going to the TV towers. We checked our radios and established a check-in schedule. If I didn't check in, he was to alert the military, utilizing our direct radio link to both the Israeli and southern Lebanese forces. I headed my car back along the road that would take me past the border and safety to the no-man's-land above the Litani River— toward the looming guns of Beufort Castle. I was questioning myself pretty hard by now: Was I being a macho fool, going this far north myself? Should I wait for a squad of soldiers to be my backup? Unfortunately, that might take days, what with the frenzied preparations underway for whatever the Israeli military was planning for Beufort Castle. With a deep sigh, I kept driving as if some force was keeping my foot on the accelerator instead of the brake. But my foot wasn't *too* much on the accelerator. Colonel Yourm had advised me to drive slower as I moved north, to reduce the dust plume from the car and hopefully avoid attracting PLO patrols. This was my first trip to the TV towers because I wasn't in Lebanon when they were installed. I was navigating by a crude map drawn for me by the station operator, feeling every inch like some treasure hunter from *Raiders of the Lost Ark*. I kept a close eye on the odometer because the map noted miles, and this was not downtown Los Angeles with street signs on every corner. I had to watch for the curves, hills, and big rocks with unusual shapes scribbled on my treasure map, or I might find myself pulling up to a PLO checkpoint just south of Beirut. Taking the colonel's advice seriously, I was crawling along at about fifteen miles per hour. Come to think of it, this part *was* like Los Angeles freeways— during rush hour.

Finally, I came around a turn and spotted the narrow dirt road that wound up to Maroun er Ras and our tower. I was very mindful of the menacing structure of the deadly Beufort Castle and the prying eyes of the PLO gunners. Had they seen my dust plume? Would they take any action if they had? This was pounding in my mind as I crept at a tortoise's pace up the hill, willing the car's dust cloud to settle down. When I reached the top of the hill, I almost forgot the danger as I got my first glimpse of the view. It was gorgeous. Off to my left, the ocean's green and blue hues shimmered; whitecaps lapping the finely sanded beach added to the postcard view. To my right, the lush and fertile Beqaa Valley stretched toward Beirut. Sadly, the rich farmland that had once produced fruit and vegetables now grew terrorists. This thought returned me to the business at hand.

A rickety fence marked the perimeter of the tower. I slowly drove to the small structure housing the generators and scanned the area for any sign of life. For a few minutes I sat in my car surveying the hill and the road I had just come up. Then I realized: I'm sitting on top of the hill in a bright yellow vehicle. I might as well have a big bull's-eye on my car. So, I positioned the car as far as I could toward the ocean side of the property, which slanted down and way from the view of the castle. As I got out, I chambered a round into the Uzi and double-checked the safety to ensure it would come off quickly. I took the extra clips with me to the base of the tower. I used the shoulder strap to throw the Uzi on my back.

I quickly got the equipment out of the car and started installing the sensors. Sweating in the dust at the edge of the Holy Land, I imagined being one of the Jews returned from exile, working beside the prophet Nehemiah to rebuild the walls of Jerusalem. Their enemies mocked the effort and set out to destroy the work being done stone by stone. Uzi on my shoulder, I heard the words of Nehemiah: "The laborers who carried the loads worked with one hand and held a weapon with the other" (Neh. 4:17).

God's people would go about their business, but they would defend themselves. My own electronic version of Nehemiah's wall was half complete when the air was pierced by the high-pitched whine of a low-flying jet. My military training kicked in and I hit the deck just as an Israeli jet screamed over the hill at about five hundred feet in altitude, streaking toward a PLO stronghold in the Beqaa Valley. I lifted my head in time to see two streams of smoke shoot from the aircraft wings—missiles taking aim at their targets in the valley below. *Flash! Flash!* By the time the noise and vibrations from the blast reached me, the jet had climbed safely out of the fire zone and was racing back overhead to the safety of the ocean and the Israeli border. No sooner did the first jet peel away than a second wave of jets came thundering across the sky—then a third. For the next fifteen minutes plane after plane, missile after missile, pounded the PLO terrorist camps. I had a front-seat view of the Israelis' pent-up response to the terror war waged against them. But a thought crossed my mind: *What am I doing here, putting some Mickey Mouse early-warning system around these towers, with the missiles and firepower the PLO have? Even if they're just returning fire at the planes coming over the hill, what are they going to hit? Oh well. I'm here,* I reasoned. *I should at least finish.*

I went back to the task at hand, working like an Indy pit crew. Within two hours, the installation was complete. The radio station confirmed it was receiving the sensor signals. The test check was a success. My job was done. Time to leave, and what a relief!

"Though I Walk Through the Valley . . ."

I was loading bags into my trunk when I heard a car on the road coming up to the tower. It had pulled off the main road and stopped as if to listen or see what was going on. The bottom of the hill wasn't visible from my vantage point, so all I could do was wait. After a few minutes, the mystery car started crawling up the hill. With no friendly forces known to be in the area, that left only . . . well . . .

I radioed the station that presumed hostiles were approaching the tower. Not wanting to be a sitting duck in the car, I grabbed the extra clips and ran for some rocks overlooking the road approaching the tower. Legs shaking and hands sweaty from the run to the rocks, I peered out from behind the boulders and didn't like what I saw: four males in street clothes with weapons poking out the windows. This was definitely not a friendly patrol. It didn't take a counterterrorism expert to know these were PLO and they were looking for me. I knew if I let them get to the top of hill, I was through. I'd be outgunned, out-numbered, and holding the low ground. My only chance was to hit them before they got to the top. A sharp curve below the line of the hill offered my best opportunity. I prayed out loud and told God, *You sent me here. Now I need your help.*

From my perch, I could see the nose of the car slowly coming into view, fifty yards below. It would be difficult for them to get out and charge me with the steep slope of the hill and no cover. I held my breath and when the front half of the car was exposed, I laid a line of fire, starting at the front of the car and taking out the front windshield. The vehicle slammed to a halt, smoke pouring from the engine compartment. Did I hit anyone? My question was soon answered by four assault rifles opening up on my position. I returned fire, pinning them down behind the rock and their car.

While I had a momentary advantage, this was not a good situation. Time was on their side, and my ammunition would run out before theirs. My time for maneuvering was short. I desperately tried to radio the station and military: "Anyone, do you copy? Under attack!" No response. The signal was apparently not getting out from my position. Great time for the radio not to work. My mind flashed to my wife and two boys at home. Would I ever see them again? Would I wind up a prisoner to be tortured then bartered? Death or capture? I didn't like either option.

The next few minutes seemed more like days, as the gunmen systematically sent bursts of rounds my way. They were well trained; they rotated fire from their different positions. I knew it was a matter of time, with the only factors in my favor being the steep hill and their ignorance of how many foes they faced. Moving a few feet to my left, I sent a short burst of bullets toward the rocks where they were hidden, then dashed back to my right about twenty feet to send another short burst of bullets their way. This seemed to give them pause as everything got very quiet and their yelling ceased. Time was also beginning to work against them. The longer they stayed pinned down, the better the odds the South Lebanese Army or Israelis would spot them and come to my aid. As their silence continued, I knew they were planning something. And soon my fears were confirmed.

The air suddenly crackled with a heavy and systematic barrage. I couldn't even peek over the rock to see their movements because of the lead pouring toward me. I didn't want to waste bullets just pointing the Uzi over the hill and firing. No, if I had to make a last stand, I wanted bullets in my gun. They were shouting. Whatever they were saying, I knew it wasn't good for me. I finally dared to sneak a look over the rock. The four were fanning out and coming up the hill less than fifty yards away. I could almost smell their sweaty bodies. Forty yards away. As I considered my course of action, I prepared for the worst. If only an Israeli patrol had picked up the firefight and would come to my aid! The gunmen were getting closer: thirty yards . . . twenty yards. I had to make a move. Now or never isn't a cliché when I'm in someone's gun sights.

Just as I started to look over the rock for a target, a beautiful, black, and, oh, so blessed Apache gunship rose from below the hill. Just like in the movies! Nose down in attack position, the Apache circled to my right, kicking up dirt and spitting out lead; its guns letting loose the sweetest music I have ever heard. I made a mad—if gleeful—dash for the tower to get out of the line of fire, giving the Apache the freedom to use all the firepower it needed. Two minutes later, the guns suddenly fell silent. All I could hear was the whirl of the chopper blades biting the air . . . and my heart as it tried leaving my chest.

The pilot of the gunship motioned for me to take off. Gunning my car, I wondered how I was going to get down from the hill with the PLO car blocking the road. The Apache crew was way ahead of me. They simply blasted the vehicle clear over the side. Racing down the hill, I passed the bodies of the dead PLO. I confess, I had no thought of what would happen to their corpses or souls: They had wanted to kill me.

I hit the road leading south to the border, this time caring nothing about dust clouds or holes in the road. The Apache covered my escape, following me until I was within sight of the Good Fence gate. The Pearly Gates couldn't have been more welcomed at that moment. I drove into Israel, pulled over, and merely sat there. The adrenaline rush over, I was shaking on the inside and out. Eventually, this might be an exciting story to tell my future grandchildren—a big adventure from long ago—but at that moment I was nauseated, shivering, and giving tearful thanks to God for that Israeli gunship.

Deliverance

This was my first real wake-up call to the danger I was caught up in. Before, danger had been in the air but not close and personal. This time I saw death pointing right at me and realized how very near I'd come to having my life ended. I still had things I wanted to do. *Was this worth it? Could I really make a difference?* All of these thoughts raced through my mind as I sat by the side of the road outside Metulla for what seemed to be an eternity. In my rearview mirror, I could see the sign at the Good Fence: "Weapons shall be beaten into plow shares and there shall be no more war." How far we seemed to be from the fulfillment of Isaiah's prophecy. With a deep sigh, I started the car and headed for a long, cold shower and a chance to put this day behind me.

Showers are one of God's greatest creations. By the time I headed down to the hotel restaurant I felt 100 percent better.

Colonel Yourm joined me. "Are you OK?" he asked. As I related the events of the day, he said, "We picked up your radio call and dispatched the gunship." "Thank you" was about all I could manage. Concerned about my state of mind after such an ordeal, my friend sat with me, listened, and shared. We talked about how this experience was something his troops faced every day; life meant more than merely staying alive, and the disease of apathy is far more deadly than the danger of the PLO. By the time we finished dinner, any doubts about my mission were answered. I would stay the course.

Yourm asked me about my schedule for the next day. *Hopefully, something without bullets,* I thought to myself but said aloud, "I'll probably go to the studio and check on the equipment, but I'm open." "Good," he said. "I have someone I want you to meet."

A Man of Vision

We left the restaurant and walked up the street to the command post. There he introduced me to a tall, distinguished gentleman who appeared to be in his midsixties. "Phil, I'd like you to meet Herman Wouk." I instantly knew who he was: my wife's favorite author. He held out his hand and spoke with a deep voice that radiated confidence. "How are you?" His handshake surprised me. I was expecting the soft hand of a writer, but instead he squeezed my fingers with a hand of steel. Wouk was in Israel researching what would eventually become the best-selling novels *The Hope* and *The Glory* that span the time from Israel's war for independence in 1948 to the bombing of the Iraqi nuclear reactor in 1981. I later learned Wouk was a man of deep faith, devoted to the Torah and passionate about the importance of religious roots to American Jews. This trip was part of his own spiritual journey.

Yourm asked if I'd be interested in taking Wouk into Lebanon with me the next day so he could see firsthand what had happened to southern Lebanon. I immediately agreed. I rushed to my room and called my wife in the States. "You'll never guess who I just met!" For security reasons and to avoid undue worry, I didn't discuss case matters or close calls over the phone with my wife. So we chatted excitedly about the prospects of my spending a day with her favorite writer. The evening had restored me, and I drifted to sleep with a special dose of thankfulness.

The next morning at 8:00 a.m., I picked up Herman Wouk. As he walked toward me like a man on a mission, I must admit I was a little nervous. I was neither the student nor the reader that my wife was, and she had built this man up to the point that I was afraid to open my mouth. However, despite his commanding presence, Wouk was completely disarming. His smiling eyes instantly turned my intimidation into trust. I was set at ease, and I knew he would be easy to talk to.

After a few more minutes of getting acquainted, we got in the car and headed for the Good Fence gate. The guards had been alerted that I would have a passenger, and as we approached the gate, it opened as if we'd uttered a magic word.

Today there'd be no venturing too far north. As we surveyed shot-up towns and the scarred countryside ravaged by the PLO, we talked of life, the world, and the future of mankind. Herman Wouk had a very keen insight into the future and was able to weave history into his vision of that future. Even though his most noted books were about war and conflict, I learned quickly that he was a positive man with hope for the days ahead, if only people could see evil for what it was and act against it. Wouk's desire to somehow stop the cycle of violence and educate the world on what was really happening in the Middle East went straight to my heart. He talked of the centuries-old division between Arabs and Jews and his hope for an awakening of the human spirit of compassion and forgiveness. I could only say, "Amen."

The day passed too quickly. I didn't want to leave the presence of this very special man. But as darkness approached, we left behind the destruction of Lebanon and discussions of peace and pulled through the Good Fence gate. Back at the command headquarters, Herman and I shook hands and parted ways. His books may have reached and touched millions, but it was the man himself who reached and moved me.

I left, feeling very blessed to have been in this place in this hour and to experience both the good and the bad of the previous two days. It crystallized my thoughts on life and death, particularly as they pertained to the struggle we were in; these were thoughts that carry down to the present in our battle against today's terrorists. In the Old Testament, God laid before the people—and before us—a choice: the path of life or the path of death. The PLO terrorists hunting me in 1982—and their like-minded comrades targeting us today—chose darkness. Their choice, their idol, is death. I chose light, having come to grasp fully for the first time on that hillside that to gain one's life one must be willing to lose it in service to others. To win the fight against the darkness of terror, we must champion the light. The Israelis understood this choice given by their God. They celebrate it, and I join in their toast.

L'chaim! To life!

The Iranian Connection, Part 1

THE ERUPTION OF CELEBRATION in Palestinian streets on the morning of September 11 was no surprise to me. I knew attacks the magnitude of 9/11 had been a gleam in the eye of terrorists, secretly meeting for years within the PLO refugee camps scattered across Lebanon. Long before bin Laden and al-Qaeda, the wicked minds of the schemers dreamed of the destruction of Western democracies and our freedom of religion. At their center, stoking the flames of hatred, was Iran and its pit-bull group, Hezbollah—the A-team of violent terrorist groups. Back when bin Laden was still enjoying life as a billionaire's son, Iran and its surrogates, including Hezbollah, were already creeping worldwide, establishing a foothold in countries around the globe, aiming to tighten a noose around our necks. This was—and is—a fight to the finish, to the death. But the fight isn't always ugly. In fact, sometimes it can be downright beautiful and sexy, as I discovered in 1988, when I got a telephone call.

By this time, each time my phone rang I wondered where the call would lead. Was it a friend? A harmless client? Or someone trying to lure me to my destruction? This may sound melodramatic, but thanks to my alignment with the southern Lebanese forces, I was now a PLO target of choice. It would use any means, even posing as friends, to lure me to a place where I could be disposed of without a trace.

Fortunately, this call was from an old friend raised in the Middle East but now in business in the States. The friend—I'll call him Richard—sounded anxious. He had a problem in London and had heard about my station there, with high-level police and military contacts throughout Great Britain. He needed to meet with me as soon as possible. Richard wouldn't discuss the matter over the phone, so I cleared my calendar and by breakfast was winging my way to Seattle, where he was located. *Why the urgency?* I wondered on the way to his office. I also wondered, *Do I have the knowledge and resources to complete the assignment, whatever it is?*

Soon, over a cup of strong coffee in his spacious, well-appointed office, Richard spilled his story. "I'm a consultant to many Persian Gulf leaders," he confided. "And now one of them—a king—is being blackmailed." His Highness had been involved in a romantic dalliance with a woman he knew as Renee Losson. She supposedly had a child, a son, by the king and was now living in London. However, the king had never seen the child and wanted to determine if the boy even existed. Our assignment: Locate the woman, follow her, see if she led us to a child, and if so, recover the child. Seemed simple and straightforward enough. But never forget the first rule of investigation: Never assume anything.

Actually, that's the second rule. The first rule is get the retainer first. Richard arranged a wire transfer for the twenty-five-thousand-dollar retainer, and we got down to business. I reviewed all Richard's records and made copies of all the pertinent information. Well, not quite *all* the pertinent information: Richard forgot to mention that another agency had worked on this case for months with little result other than Renee discovering she was being watched.

Departing Seattle, I contacted my people in Los Angeles to

get them rolling. They ran Renee's name through all the sources and computers we had available, both in the United States and in Europe. I also called Robert, the agent in charge of our station in London, giving him a possible address for Renee and instructing him to develop a profile on the residence.

My emotions seesawed on my flight back to Los Angeles. One minute I'd be elated that I would soon be speeding to London, and the next minute I was second-guessing myself. *How can a farm boy from Missouri hope to solve a royal mess halfway around the world?* Fortunately, I had been raised in a very strong, loving family and taught from my earliest days to have a strong sense of self-worth and faith in my ability. By the time I landed in Los Angeles, I was ready to take on the world—or at least a royal mistress—and was looking forward to being on the ground in London.

A Needle in a Haystack

My first clue to the case's complication came the next morning while reviewing printouts from the searches we had started. Renee Losson didn't exist, at least, according to those printouts. This raised a big, billowing red flag. If I find no information on a person who I was told was in her late thirties, the subject is either a backwoods, antisocial hermit, she's assumed someone else's identity, or she's created a fake persona. Because backwoods hermits don't usually have romances with Middle Eastern royalty, we suspected Renee was not who she said she was. We kept searching, but there weren't any hits on her name. Nothing—no credit cards, no bank accounts, no driver's license. She was a mirage. As I pored over page after page of reports, I tried to see into Renee's mind: *Who are you? Why are you hiding? Who are you running from? What is your secret?*

Further mystery awaited me on the other end of a scrambled phone connection to my station chief in London. "You know that address you gave me, Phil? It's in one of the most expensive parts of the city. The home's worth at least 2 million dollars." Robert went on to say his people had made a middle of the night run on the trash bins at the residence and found mail addressed to Renee Losson. So she *did* exist. But how was she maintaining a $2-million house without any visible means of support? We discussed an operational plan, including setting up surveillance on three addresses in London; we knew of a residence on Oak Tree Road near Saint John's Wood in northwest London, but we also found addresses connected to Renee on Kensington Avenue and Chiswick Gardens. We were going to need more agents and more digging than I originally thought. "I'll be in London within twenty-four hours," I told Robert.

Back in Seattle, Richard had briefed me that Renee might have family ties in France and Germany, so my next two calls were to the station chiefs in Paris and Bonn—Jean and Anselm. Speaking on a secure phone line, I told Jean about the subject and informed him that Renee and her associates traveled to France and were supposedly involved in arms, drug deals, and possibly had terrorist connections. "Pull out all the stops on this one," I said. "Move with all speed possible." When I got through to Anselm, I gave him all the background and the reason for our interest in Germany. "We believe the subject has an adopted son living in Düsseldorf, but according to our information he denies any knowledge of her. Something doesn't add up." I instructed Anselm to start a background and activity check on the young Iranian adopted son, Ali.

In this business I had to be ready to move on a dime—or a shilling, as the case may be. Some private investigators even carry a travel bag in their cars in case they have to jump on an airplane while following a suspect. I had only a couple of hours before my flight to meet with my Los Angeles team and explain the work needed to support the operation in London. We also had many other ongoing cases, but I was blessed to have a well-qualified team running the home office while I got the fun job of globe-trotting. Part of the daily duty of the home office was to review intelligence reports from our field operatives around the world and to ensure that any information we needed to pass on to the government agencies was handled in a timely manner. My gang would also keep me informed of any crucial reports as I traveled. Knowing the office was in good hands, I packed with great excitement. I love Europe and I love to travel. I even love being at the airport! And certainly, I love a good mystery.

The British Airlines flight was smooth, and my first-class seat made a comfy bed. By the time I woke up, we were already on our descent into London's Heathrow airport. I was met at the gate by one of my agents, a supervisor at customs. Lloyd walked me through customs, and in less than thirty minutes we were heading for the hotel. I enjoyed every minute of the ride, soaking up the sights and drinking in the mystery of this, the city that spawned Arthur Conan Doyle's Sherlock Holmes.

Lloyd had set me up at the Kensington Park Hotel, near the center of our operation. I checked in and arranged to meet Lloyd and my station chief Robert in the lobby an hour and a half later.

Still wired, as I always am in Europe, I was in the lobby within an hour, checking out the shops. When my people arrived, we settled ourselves at one of the hotel bars, and they brought me up to date on what they had learned. They had visually identified the woman who lived there under the name Renee Losson, and she appeared to fit the description the client had given us. The subject also had been spotted coming and going from the residence but never with a child in tow. Renee was going out late at night as well, hitting the trendy after-hours clubs of London. I informed Robert that our client had authorized surveillance 24/7, and if Renee got on an airplane we were to follow her anywhere in the world. I continued, "At all costs, don't get burned! We can't let her know we are on her. Our team has to have enough agents to be versatile, and we must always have a female agent on hand if she goes out at night." The female agent could follow the subject into the restroom and perhaps have an opportunity to start a conversation. If we were lucky, she might even be able to build a relationship.

The residence was a short distance from my hotel, and we decided to go by the house so I could get a firsthand look. The area is popular with foreign diplomats, and as we approached her street, we could see ample evidence of affluence and elegance: mansions with palatial exteriors and opulent gardens, dramatically illuminated at night. Many had gated walls secluding them from the street—not so at Renee's house, thankfully. As we drove slowly past the residence, I was able to see the large double front doors from the street and I could make out some of the windows. We parked just past the house, and I assessed the situation. It might be possible to see through some of the windows if the blinds were open. I instructed Robert to ensure that all the surveillance teams had cameras with telephoto lenses in case they were able to get close-ups of her. The bad news? Street parking was going to be a nightmare for our surveillance teams. The house was very close to the street and had two cars in a garage area in front. The street itself was Twiggy-thin and didn't allow parking on both sides. We were going to have to be very creative in finding locations for the teams to park.

After looking at the street and finding there were no side streets the subject could leave on, we realized we could place the agents at the ends of the road and pick her up when she left.

However, if she left with someone else, we might miss seeing her in another car. We settled on having at least one agent in place to view the house at all times so we could know when she was outside; the agent might also be able to get pictures for positive identification. The local team had already determined the trash pickup days and put in place a detail responsible for beating the garbage pickup on Thursday mornings. The first raid had already given us many interesting leads on her activities and involvements and confirmed that she wasn't using a shredder. Over time, Renee's trash became very interesting and informative. Later, I'd remember the old saying, "If it's too good to be true, it probably isn't."

The Stakeout

At the first gray of the London dawn, I made my way to the subject's location. We had two agents on the scene, with one parked on the sidewalk at an angle across from the house. They could see the front door and gate but not be in the normal view of someone exiting the residence. I could see that our agent in front of the house would have to move throughout the day because of narrow streets and nosy neighbors. If our information was correct—that Renee liked to party at night—she was probably a late riser. Still, we couldn't take the chance of missing her.

Back at the hotel, I made some calls to Scotland Yard contacts to see if anything had turned up on my request for background on the mysterious Renee Losson. My associates weren't in yet, so I settled in at the lobby restaurant to have a late breakfast and people-watch. At about 1:00 p.m. I received a call that there was activity in the residence. I scurried back to the scene.

Getting out of the car, I took a stroll down the street to get a closer look, cloaked by thick fog. I approached the address from the opposite side of the street—walking slowly, trying to look English, and hoping I didn't run into friendly neighbors. Then, emerging out of the mist and gliding toward the trash bin was an attractive brunette with long, silky hair.

She gave me a look of curiosity, and her face held the start of a smile. I knew my American accent would take a lot of explaining. I didn't have a good story prepared, and I also didn't want her to get a good look at me in case I needed to have a "chance meeting" with her at some point during the investigation.

When I got back to the car, I learned that the agent across from her residence had gotten a number of pictures of her; now we could run her image through Interpol and see if anything came up. By now, my Scotland Yard contacts had called to say they still didn't have anything on her; she was living in their city and was apparently a person of means but didn't seem to exist. This made the Yard nervous.

With the facts we had on Renee—or whatever her name was—it was clear she was involved in more than trying to hide a child from the father. She had to have a lot of income to support her lifestyle and the house. The property was in the name of an offshore company she controlled, and there was no lien against the house; she—or a cohort—had paid millions for the property, in cash.

Activating
the German GSG9

I DECIDED TO GO to Germany and meet with our station chief, Anselm Weygold, who had spent fifteen years with GSG9, Germany's special forces unit; he was a founding member of that elite force. Weygold also had strong ties to German intelligence, which had a very active unit working Middle Eastern terrorist groups. If Renee was in cahoots with any terrorist-supporting country or terrorist group, Lemmie—as his friends called him— was our best hope for quickly surfacing the connection.

In the early '80s, our nation was woefully ignorant of evolving terrorist methods and techniques, such as car and suitcase bombs. A report from Lemmie might include inside information on a particular terrorist car bombing, including detailed diagrams of how the vehicles had been fitted with explosives. I would pass this information to the bomb squads in Los Angeles, which would then share it with federal agencies. Any information we could give local agents helped prepare them for dangers they could someday face. In fact, a catastrophic failure to prepare by the German government led directly to the creation of GSG9.

GSG9 was Germany's response to the Palestinian terrorist attacks on the Israeli athletes at the 1972 Munich Olympics and a response to the German authorities' mind-numbing ineptitude in handling the situation. To learn how *not* to handle a hostage situation, rent the chilling, Oscar-winning documentary *One Day in September.* For example, TV cameras were allowed to broadcast security team movements directly into the hijackers' rooms; police units abandoned attack positions; there was virtually no communication capability between officers; German officials refused help from the Mossad. In the end, the authorities formulated an attack strategy almost guaranteed to allow the terrorists time to kill their hostages. In the end, the eleven Israeli athletes were dead. "They're all gone," said a mournful Jim McKay of ABC, "all of them." Still, out of the ashes of that horrific experience and the resulting national humiliation rose one of the best counterterrorist units in the world. One of the reasons for its success is organization and training. Although there was considerable distrust between the Israelis and Germans after the massacre, Israel put distrust aside and was fully involved in the original training and organization of GSG9, sharing Israeli intelligence know-how and tactics. Israel deserves much credit for the unit's subsequent success.

A No-Nonsense Approach

GSG9's response to terrorist attacks or other national security incidents differed from the way the United States responded at the time, and I confess the German model is much more effective. Even though GSG9 was a military unit headed by military officers, it was taken out of the military chain of command. The unit commander took his orders directly from the chancellor. In the United States at that time, any response decision had to worm through a maze of time-consuming in-boxes, both military and civilian. The Germans could be on the scene and solving the problem before American forces even got the go-ahead. Also, GSG9 was formed into five-man units with each team having air, sea, and land experts. A unit was on standby around the clock. Within one hour of a call from the chancellor, a plane could be in the air carrying the team to the hot zone. Thanks to all the competing, turf-protecting services and politicians, the United States would not begin catching this effective counterterrorism vision until after 9/11.

GSG9 was my kind of unit. Even though I wasn't German, it gave me great pride to be around the unit members, to realize they were ready to go into any situation and expect to come back with the job done.

On the way to Lemmie's home, we stopped at intelligence headquarters and put Renee's profile and picture into the German system. From there, it also would be fed to Interpol. I was reminded of my first visit to Interpol several years earlier at its old headquarters in Paris. I was an American ex-cop turned private eye who, like all Americans, watched too much TV. To me, Interpol was a state-of-the-art, superpolice agency watching every movement, particularly in Europe.

To my surprise and dismay, I discovered Interpol wasn't watching every move. In fact, it hardly had the capacity to watch *anybody's* move. As I walked through the different sections of its headquarters, I was muttering, "This *can't* be the world-famous Interpol!" When I got to the intelligence section, I expected to see massive computers—whirling, humming monsters just waiting to be fed a name; within a few seconds, I assumed, they would spit out every last detail of the subject's life. Wrong. Instead of an array of top-of-the-line computers, I found a row of large file-card tubs. I had to rotate the tubs to get to the letter of the alphabet I wanted. Once there, I manually flipped through for an index card handwritten with the subject's information . . . yes, handwritten. No wonder it took so long to get information from Interpol. An average public library at the time had a more modern system.

(Today, I am glad to report, advanced technology has finally found its way to Interpol. Of course, many of the countries with agents attached to Interpol are the same countries who support terrorists and their causes, but that's for another time.)

As you can imagine, I wasn't expecting a quick response on Renee from Interpol. I knew the Germans were going to act much faster.

In what seemed like only a few minutes, we pulled off the autobahn and into Mönchengladbach, outside Düsseldorf. I was still catching my breath and loosening my face muscles when we entered Lemmie's spacious home. We took a dip in his indoor swimming pool, and I got my first whiff of the delectable venison Lemmie's wife was preparing for dinner.

The next day we began receiving intelligence about Renee's adopted son. Here was the summary I read:

> Ali [name deleted] was borne in 1966 in Iran and lives in a one-room apartment on Hansaallee Street in Düsseldorf. He attends Albrecht Dürer Vocational School located at Furstenwall 100. On occasion, the subject visits a nearby bistro with two of his classmates. Agents made contact with a teacher who describes Ali as an outsider who tends to be reserved, inconspicuous, and less communicative than others in his class. Through Iranian contacts in Düsseldorf, we determined that upper-class Iranians congregate every Wednesday afternoon at a bar called Nachrichtentreff on Konigsalolee Düsseldorf. Inquiries were made but neither the subject nor the subject's mother is known by those who frequent the bar.

We got lucky when we contacted the personnel manager at the hotel where Ali worked. He related that Ali had been a German citizen since 1980, having come from the United Kingdom. His immigration was handled by an attorney who we believed had been in contact with Renee in England. We learned that Renee came to Düsseldorf in February 1988 and stayed at the Intercontinental Düsseldorf for several days. She was described as an attractive woman in her late thirties, fashionably dressed and wearing expensive jewelry. She gave the appearance of substantial wealth. She used a different name and address while she was at the hotel. It would not be the last alias we would uncover.

I said to myself, *Where is your wealth from, Renee? Drugs? Arms? Other rich lovers? Or are you a weapon of the Iranian radical terrorists?*

I worked out an operational plan for Lemmie to continue digging on the German front. As I flew back to Heathrow, I wondered if this tough and tenacious German would give me the information I needed to close in on the beautiful, elusive Renee Losson.

chapter 12

The Iranian Connection, Part 2

ARRIVING BACK IN LONDON, I was met by my station chief, who again walked me through customs. On the ride back to the hotel he briefed me on what I had missed. Apparently, we rummaged up a major break in the case—literally; the information came straight from Renee's trash. We recovered a purchase order for F-14 spare parts to be shipped to Iran. The tricky part was that they were to be shipped as tractor tires in an attempt to get past the U.S. ban on exports of military parts to Iran. This supported information I had just received from a confidential informant in Germany, indicating Renee and her boyfriend had been working on an arms deal since March of the previous year through a middleman named Robert Strausmann. The Iranian shopping list also included sixteen F-5 aircraft and parts for them. This list had been around for awhile; and as our investigation expanded, we found links to an attempt to exchange F-5s for American and Western hostages still in Iran's control.

There was also a domestic political angle. We uncovered an attempt by Iranian agents to get approval for the sale by using the political leverage of people connected to then-Vice President Bush during his 1988 presidential campaign. In return, hostages would be released and Bush the Elder would receive a positive push for his election bid. Remember, this was even after the arms-for-hostages exposure of the early Reagan years and the alleged October-surprise deal supposedly made between Iran and Reagan's 1980 campaign—alleged but never proved.

This time, though, it was a no-go. One of the middlemen in the deal had access to Bush, but even so, he was turned down. Later, after the election, the arms dealers discussed trying to blackmail the new president, threatening that if he wouldn't authorize the sale, they were going to release to the press that he had been involved in an arms-for-hostages deal. The blackmail attempt didn't go far.

The Iranian wish list was very detailed, and other information revealed the Iranian intent to also purchase F-5Es from Chile or elsewhere, along with strategies for fooling the United States and the international community into thinking the warplanes really weren't for Iran. It's important to note the extent to which rogue nations will go—and are going—to hide their weapons-buying activities. These nations and terrorist groups, like Hezbollah and al-Qaeda, have only gotten more sophisticated in the years since. Unlike what some critics of President George W. Bush seem to think, Saddam Hussein wasn't likely to purchase his nuclear materials with a personal check.

The Big Picture

I decided to bring all our agents together to assess what we had before us and hopefully avoid blundering into an international mess.

We knew we were dealing with shady characters, but just how dangerous were they? We now knew they were involved with illegal arms sales, hiding sources of income, and using aliases to avoid attention. They had contacts—mostly Iranian—

all over the world. The supposedly adopted son in Germany was acting more like a sleeper terrorist than someone acclimating to a new homeland. There were ties to southern California; money was regularly wired to accounts there. The transfers were under different names, but all were controlled by Renee. Meanwhile, she was traveling around the world, including trips to the Philippines, a known breeding ground for Eastern terrorist groups with connections to the radical Islamic terrorists of Iran and the Middle East.

We scrutinized and debated every detail. We also discussed the information we were getting from the trash runs: a trove of documents, faxes, telexes, and letters. In fact, it was almost too much information, especially in light of Renee's background and her illegal activities. I was concerned she was planting material for us to see. If so, why? We had to be very careful that she wasn't pulling the strings on our investigation, sending us on wild-goose chases to divert us from her real activities. The arms and drugs could be a revenue-enhancing diversion from her ultimate task: building an international terrorist network and linking the Islamic terrorists from the Middle East to the rest of the world.

We needed to get closer. We had developed an Iranian informant who was in the same social circle as Renee. I met this informant, whom I'll call Hussein, to develop a plan to test Renee and determine what we could find out. Hussein remarked that Renee was very smart and the word on the street was to avoid involvement with her. I told Hussein I wanted to go with him to meet her. He felt that because there were a lot of foreigners, including Americans, in the after-hours clubs, my presence wouldn't be a red flag to her.

Renee's nightlife was very active. She hit the town three to four nights a week, so we had a good chance of finding her in the next day or so. The following night, a Friday, seemed a solid bet.

We kept the surveillance on all three residences, and the activities of our subject seemed pretty normal—except that some of Renee's visitors were known by Scotland Yard to have criminal ties. Meanwhile, I had Lemmie digging in Germany to find out who Ali really was and if he was the adopted or biological son of Renee. Agents in his supposed birthplace of Iran were looking for his birth certificate. We explored the possibility that Ali was the hidden son. However, the royal son we were looking for would be twelve or thirteen, while Ali was twenty-four. The more we were finding out about Renee and her deceitful ways, the more likely it seemed her whole story to our client about bearing his son was nothing more than simple extortion. Questions continued piling up faster than answers.

Face-to-Face

We picked one of the clubs Renee was known to frequent, tucked away on Crawford Street. After a late dinner with my Iranian informant, we arrived at the Crawford Street club about 2:30 a.m. We found a table near the dance risers with a good view of the room and the door. The main room was small enough we were able to see all the hundred or so people already there, along with groups of bettors huddled around gaming tables in the back.

About an hour later, Renee made her entrance. The way she was greeted, it was obvious she was well known at the club. She glided around the room, greeting many of the patrons, most of whom were Middle Eastern or Iranian. She was not with her boyfriend, which made the contact more probable because our indications were that the boyfriend was very paranoid and overly suspicious. Later, I'd find out why.

Renee took a table with another man and woman she knew, near enough so that we had eye contact. I wondered if it might be possible to exchange pleasantries with her and perhaps even get her phone number. It might work, but with a shrewd case like Renee, I'd have to be very careful. After about thirty minutes, I managed to catch her eye long enough to give me an excuse to have drinks sent to her table. Hussein went over and introduced himself, and the other couple at her table left. Hussein gestured at our table, and she got up and came toward me, a slight smile parting her lips. I must say a lot of thoughts danced through my mind, but fortunately the loudest one was, *She might be smarter than you.* I needed to get information from her, not the other way around.

Hussein introduced me as an American investor working in Europe. He told her I was in London for a few days to visit friends. "I'm showing Phil the night life," he said, casually mentioning that he might be tied up for the next night or two. She circled the bait. As we talked about life in England, I noticed she kept herself aware of who was coming and going but did so very discreetly. At the same time, she was probing with questions about my life and work, trying, I think, to find a hole in my story. When I asked about her work, she avoided a direct answer and said she handled family investments. I knew from recent intelligence she was looking for $90 million to finance the aircraft spare parts purchase for Iran. In fact, some of her questions attempted to gauge my level of funds and what kind of investments I was interested in.

She was a very intelligent, engaging woman—fun to talk to, despite everything I knew about her. By the end of the evening, and despite many good reasons to the contrary, I liked this woman. *So she's a terrorist,* the insidious voice of temptation whispered. *Nobody's perfect.*

Sunrise approached. While Renee seemed to just be getting warmed up, I was fading fast. We started to part ways. "Give me a call if you have some time or need a guide," she said, handing me a piece of paper. I was not only flirting with disaster; I was exchanging telephone numbers with it.

On the way back to the hotel, Hussein and I debated how to proceed. On one hand, going out with Renee could gain me crucial information. On the other hand, argued Hussein, she was too connected and the potential danger of exposure would be greater than what I might hope to learn. In the end, I submitted to wisdom and Hussein's greater experience with beautiful Iranian spies. "You win," I said as we reached the hotel.

I collapsed on the bed and slept through the whole day. That evening I met with the station chief and a pair of my agents. Before I left to go back to the States, I wanted to assess what we knew and try to notice any patterns or possible answers to what Renee was up to. Too bad I couldn't just take that phone number in my pocket, call, and ask.

We had put together a list of names of those who had visited her or were connected in some way. Most of the principals were Iranian, but there were two or three Lebanese. When we took into account her connection to the current radical regime in Iran, this could be another signal of terrorist activity. At this point, we couldn't figure out exactly what they were up to. They hadn't taken any overt action but could be planning one. Many of her associates were involved in illegal activities, particularly her boyfriend Mohammed, who was looking over his shoulder day and night. We knew it was going to take time to get answers, so we decided to continue all the different aspects of the investigation in England, France, Germany, the United States, the Philippines, and Iran. I worked out the operation plan for London with the station chief, then booked a flight back to Los Angeles.

European Roots, American Soil

I WAS HAVING mixed feelings about leaving Europe, even though I had many reasons to go home. Europe felt like a second home and still does; I love to stroll the cities and villages, admiring buildings that have been standing for centuries. I thrive on finding narrow, tourist-free streets and discovering hidden jewels of history barely mentioned in the books. People in Europe think I'm European—until I open my mouth and the American Midwest comes pouring out—and I love that feeling of fitting in.

When they find out I'm a private investigator, any distaste they may have for Americans disappears, and the questions start. "What's it like being a private eye?" "What are you investigating now?" "Ever investigate any movie stars?" American TV's version of the private eye has embedded itself in the hearts and minds of people around the world. In fact, there's a little of the private eye in every one of us; we all want to know secrets no one else knows. We all want to solve the unsolvable. And some of us think we could be that slick and confident super agent we see on TV and in the movie theater.

But for all my reluctance at leaving the dash and romance of Europe, for all the theatrical adventures, I knew this was no TV show. Knowing what I knew about the spread of Iranian-connected radicals, I could almost feel terrorists boarding the plane with me for the flight to America. I'd be greeted at LAX by one of my agents. Would the bad guys be greeted by their agents as well?

Trying to Put It Together

We weren't long in the air before I cracked open the case file again. I had learned the third or fourth review of the facts sometimes brings new insight. I was looking for that one thread that was out of place: some action or movement that would reveal the real purpose of this group's activities. It had an apparent interest in several countries because it was building assets around the globe. The group also was dealing in arms, and Iran was a known breeding ground for a radical Islamic viewpoint that advocated violence to change the course of the world. Another factor that pointed to terrorist activities was the drug trafficking, a method used by the Islamic terrorist groups, as noted earlier, both to raise money for their violence and to decay the internal fabric of a country at the same time.

Up to this point, most of the Western world held the view that the terrorist mission was to take over the Middle East and then they'd be happy. But what if the reports I read from the Lebanese terrorist training camps in 1978—consistent with what we were now finding in this Iranian investigation—were true? The common thread was starting to look more like an international web. The facts contradicted the assumption that terrorists were interested only in the Middle East. The real purpose was not a takeover in the Middle East but the Far East as well and, eventually, the United States. If so, terrorists would need dedicated followers in all parts of the world. Intelligence agencies already knew about the patience of the Iranians and other promoters of terrorism. They would take years, if necessary, to put followers in place and then unleash them at the most opportune time. I read through all the surveillance reports, the list of visitors, and the papers gleamed from the 4:00 a.m. trash runs. Nothing new grabbed me, so I prepared for a long rest as the plane flew across the Atlantic Ocean.

Back in my North Hollywood office on Monday morning, I was fighting a losing battle with jet lag, "Was it really necessary to leave Europe?" I muttered to myself. Still, it was a beautiful southern California day. I decided to make the best of it.

I looked at a stack of reports, faxes, and telexes my assistant had arranged on my desk in order of importance. Claire, a British transplant and criminologist, was the corporate liaison with all the agents on the case, as well as with our royal client. She had worked for the home office in London and knew a lot of the top people in government there, including the police commissioner. She was lovely as well as tough-minded; Claire would review all the files and give me a daily summary with a priority list. Sitting at my office conference table, I would occasionally look at the wall across from my desk at the eight-by-twelve-foot world map with bold country colors jumping out of the blue ocean. Anytime my mind started to wander to the next French bistro I might eat in, Claire's voice would cut through my reverie like the Germans penetrating the Maginot Line: "Phil, where are you?"

Finally, I hit pay dirt. I had in my hands a telex that read:

CONFIDENTIAL

On April 15, we received information that relates to the alleged exchange of F-15As for hostages. The enclosed Exhibit 15 contains documents relating to the role played by a supposed C.I.A. operative in Nicaragua [whom I will call Robert Morgan]. The documents show that Morgan was part of an attempt to route 16 planes through Chile and possibly Iran. This event became a major factor in the U.S. presidential election, when it appeared that the parties involved

were threatening George Bush, stating that they would contend the
Reagan Administration had authorized another "arms for hostages"
deal after the Contragate scandal. Any such involvement was heat-
edly denied by George Schultz in a public address that pre-empted
the threatened blackmail. We have determined that the "Mr. M"
referred to in the interview with Mr. Morgan was Mohammed,
Renee's boyfriend. This puts her in the middle of the action.

I hardly had time to digest this material when I heard over the
intercom: "Urgent call from London." It was my station chief.
"Phil? We've just received confirmed information that Renee is
going to be leaving the country for Los Angeles, then on to
Hawaii and the Philippines." He said she was leaving London
within twenty-four hours, and he had agents frantically working
on her flight schedule. "Great work," I said. "Have a male and
female team follow her to the airport and get on the plane with
her to Los Angeles." Renee had been known to buy a ticket, go
to the boarding lounge, walk down the ramp, leave the plane a
few minutes later, and take another flight to a different country.
Still, LA seemed a safe bet since she had contacts and family in
the area and usually stayed with them. "I'll have a team at the
airport to pick up surveillance when she arrives."

Claire hurriedly scheduled a briefing with the Los Angeles
station chief and the head of our field investigation teams, and a
short time later we were in the conference room laying out the
facts on the case. I needed our Los Angeles team to understand
the importance and sensitivity of the case. We didn't have room
for even one mistake.

We knew Renee flew British Airways on many other flights,
and we planned on her arriving at the LAX international terminal
and clearing customs there. Fortunately, through some security
consulting I had done at LAX (see chap. 16), I had contacts in customs and relationships across the board at the airport. I knew we

would be able to monitor her coming through customs, so we wouldn't have trouble spotting her in the crowd that would pour out of customs. I informed the team I would be at the terminal, but because she knew what I looked like, I would wear a disguise and stay out of her sight. We mapped out the terminal and the placement of the agents' vehicles, covering the possibility that she might be met by someone who parked in the garage and would leave from the east end of the structure instead of the front of the terminal. For the arrival, I wanted four cars outside the terminal and three agents inside to begin following her when she came up the customs ramp to the waiting area. The three agents inside, two of them females, would subsequently join the cars to operate as spotters for the driver. As backup, I arranged to have our Jet Ranger helicopter in the air for the arrival and to ensure we didn't lose her coming out of the airport. Our pilot was an off-duty Los Angeles Police Department pilot, and he could get into the air-space around LAX. The planning sessions took nearly three hours. I assigned Claire as point person to keep all team members informed of developments as they came.

As we were breaking up the meeting, the London station chief called with Renee's flight time. She was to arrive on British Airways Sunday at 4:00 p.m., giving us a little under forty-eight hours to get our act together. The real fun was going to be when she headed for Hawaii. If we couldn't determine her schedule ahead of time, the teams following her would have to be ready to travel on a moment's notice. If we could at least identify her airline, I would purchase business-class seats and keep the departure open.

Picking Up the Scent

At 2:00 p.m. Sunday we were set up and waiting at LAX. We had heard from our agents, calling from the plane, that Renee was on board; they'd have their radios on and would give us a heads-up when they came out of customs.

The plane was five minutes late, but at 5:10 p.m., Renee came out of customs and was met by a female we knew to be her sister. Luck was on our side; Renee had three bags, so her sister went to get the car while she waited in front of the terminal. We were off to a good start because we knew the sister's address in the San Fernando Valley. Within ten minutes, we were on Interstate 405 headed north toward the valley; but to our surprise, she exited on Santa Monica Boulevard, headed east to Avenue of the Stars, and pulled up at the Century City Marriott. Renee entered and checked in. No staying in the valley for her.

This development meant that on the fly we were going to have to put together a surveillance team for the hotel. Fortunately, I knew the chief of hotel security, and I was soon on the horn, tracking him down. The rooms on both sides of Renee's were already taken, but within the hour we were set up in the room directly across from hers. I called our technical genius and had him rolling to the location with pinhole and under-the-door camera equipment so we could keep tabs on who was coming and going from her room. Her sister came to the room with her, and at 7:00 p.m. the siblings ordered room service. By eight, we had the tube camera snaking under our door and focusing across the hall on Renee's suite, with a wide angle providing a good view of anyone entering or leaving the room. Sis left at 9:30, and it appeared Renee was in for the evening. We set up shifts throughout the night and arranged for the whole team to be mobile at 6:00 a.m. We would leave one agent in the room watching the video monitor, ready to notify the agents in the lobby when she started downstairs.

As I left the hotel, my concern was twofold: How long would she be in Los Angeles, and what flight would she take to Hawaii?

Hopefully, we'd get lucky again and find which airline she was leaving on. The first place we'd check was United, a particular favorite of hers in the past. Across the Atlantic in London, our agents were still working on cracking her schedule because she booked the flights from there. Despite the uncertainty, I slept peacefully that night, knowing we had put her to bed and were set to be with her whenever she moved.

And move she did. At 7:30 a.m., after ordering a rental car and enjoying breakfast in the hotel dining room, she climbed into her car and headed out, with three of our cars trailing her. Because she was familiar with Los Angeles, I figured she'd be an easy tail: none of the high speeds and quick turns of a lost tourist. Wrong. When she left the hotel, she made a right turn on Avenue of the Stars and raced south, swinging a right turn on Pico Boulevard. When she got to 405, she headed south, back toward LAX. I wondered if she was making the kind of fast getaway— as fast as LA traffic allows—that she was known for. The jam of cars kept her speed under thirty miles per hour.

I breathed a sigh of relief as she turned onto the 90 freeway, which ends at Marina Del Rey. After a left turn on Mindanao, she turned on Admiralty Way, which circles the Marina. She went about a quarter of a mile and pulled over to the side. "Hold back!" I yelled into the radio. Renee pulled out a map book. Apparently, she didn't know exactly where she was going. However, her uncertainty was going to make our job a lot harder because she would be making quick turns and backtracking if she missed a turn. Also, she could be going to countless different places among the hundreds of yachts and boats, as well as restaurants, shops, and businesses. Renee made several turns and pulled over to stop and look around. We couldn't be sure if she was really lost or looking for a tail. We always assumed the suspect was cautious, and we took a loose-tail approach; I had already called in the helicopter as backup. She finally drove to Washington Street and Venice Beach, parking right at the sand's edge. Exiting her car, she strolled north down the Venice Beach boardwalk, carrying a camera bag and purse looped over her right shoulder.

By now, it was just after eleven o'clock, and even though it was a beautiful southern California day, the sightseers were light. She wandered two blocks along the boardwalk, peering into some shops, gazing at the gulls flapping along the sand, giving every appearance of a tourist out for some sights. Four of our agents, including two females, were now in position walking in front of and behind her. We'd be able to see anyone she might meet.

Contact!

As she walked past one of the volleyball courts, there was a man of Middle Eastern descent, approximately thirty years old, sitting on a bench facing the boardwalk. As Renee approached the bench, she stopped and sat down. For a few minutes she merely looked around, using all the techniques of a well-trained operative. After assuring herself she wasn't being watched, she turned and started talking to the man on the bench. At first it was very casual, not unlike two tourists finding themselves on the same bench. But the conversation became more personal; she moved closer to him and talked in very low tones.

Unfortunately, we did not have time to get a recording team with directional distance mikes in place to hear the whole conversation. However, we were able to pick up bits and pieces from a directional mike carried by one of the agents. We heard fragments, descriptions of "training in the Middle East" and the "need to be patient." We picked up the phrases "low profile" and "don't stand out." Renee, good leader that she was, appeared to be giving her agent direction, as well as a pep talk.

After about thirty minutes, she casually pulled out an envelope from her bag, just like in the movies. We were very certain from the view provided by a high-power telephoto lens that she was passing him money. We now had the thread we were looking for, and if we pulled it very slowly and just right, we could unravel the cover Renee and her cronies were trying to build. Renee and the contact talked for another few minutes, then she got up and set off south at a very brisk pace, not even pausing to look at the Adonis-like specimens pumping iron at Muscle Beach.

I radioed two agents of the surveillance team to stay with the male subject until he went home. We needed to know who he was and where he lived. I contacted the chopper, telling the pilot to stay in the area and keep radio contact with the team following the male subject and to also stay with it until he went home. Once we nailed his identity we could start working on his contacts and determine if there were others in his sleeper cell. *This is the break we needed,* I remember thinking. *This could be a major intelligence coup that could help protect southern California in the years to come.*

Back at the office, reports were now coming like water rushing over a cataract; the thin thread of evidence was now becoming a rope—hopefully, enough rope to hang the bad guys. From an intelligence group overseas: "We obtained reliable information that Hassan Amira, a prominent Iranian businessman and connected to the regime in Tehran, is the link between Renee and Iran."

Another report came off the wire: "Both Renee and her live-in boyfriend are tied to drugs, arms, and the building of sleeper terrorist cells. They both maintain financial accounts in New York, moving large amounts of different currencies. While the boyfriend is frantic about possible MI-6 surveillance and the CIA being after him, Renee is going about a carefree lifestyle. She keeps up her high volume of commercial transactions, moving money all over the world."

Renee was proving herself to be a cool pro, not showing any signs of concern that she might be watched or caught—while taking scrupulous care to avoid both. As I ran the names of Renee's newly discovered associates through the international terrorist watch databases, the pages of terrorist connections kept building, the most sinister being those with ties to the Middle East and the vicious, disciplined, and greatly underestimated terrorist group Hezbollah. The importance of this case had now been raised to the highest level. It was going to be critical that we stay close to Renee as she traveled the world and met her terrorist sleepers. It was now time for government agencies to take over and keep on her trail. My first task tomorrow would be to transfer all the files to the Joint Terrorist Task Force in Los Angeles.

What had started out for us in Richard's Seattle office as a royal, romantic romp the facts uncovered revealed a direct threat to the security of the United States of America.

A Choice for Death

OSAMA BIN LADEN has been seared into our minds and memories, his voice and face a fixture across the media all over the world. Although unabashedly acclaimed in some circles, his birth will eventually be remembered as a very dark day for the world. Earlier I talked about choice. No greater example exists today than Osama bin Laden. He was born with brains, material abundance, and fervor; but rather than put his gifts to work for good, he has chosen to export death in an effort to compel the course of the world to his twisted way of thinking. There have always been tools of evil who try to destroy good in any way possible, but bin Laden has taken it to a higher level than any of those before him. Just as there are good people who have affected the world positively with their talents, there are those who have been groomed from childhood to destroy life.

Is it any wonder, when we look at how children in many Middle East countries are educated that they grow up with hate, and focus that hate particularly on the United States and Israel? Each morning, millions of children go off to schools where they are immersed in the Koran and brainwashed day in and day out to hate Americans and Jews. In this cynical manner, hatred becomes religious duty. I'll discuss this detestable phenomenon more fully in a later chapter, but suffice it to say that generation after generation of Islamic extremists has been so developed, many of whom now look at Osama bin Laden as a role model.

Rise of a Terrorist Mastermind

It took many years for bin Laden to become their icon and our Public Enemy Number 1. While good people rested, evil people were working in the night, quietly building their cells and putting their sleeper terrorists next door to us, ready to respond to bin Laden's call.

For me, the Osama bin Laden story dates back to the 1980s. As we tracked the rise of international terrorism through the decade, one thing was constant: Iran was fueling the machine developing the international Islamist terror network. One would think after the Iranian hostage saga, we'd keep Iran in our crosshairs. Instead, our focus during that time was on Latin America and problems in Nicaragua, Colombia, and Grenada. The battle to combat the rise of drug usage and the destruction of our inner cities, to say nothing of communism in Latin America, was consuming our minds and attention. Meanwhile the Iranians—with the help and encouragement of the Soviets—were keeping us off balance; both groups understood Americans have trouble focusing on more than one problem at a time. A lot of this is because of the way the press filters the news; we are spoon-fed with a slant tilted to the left and toward ratings-grabbing stories, causing a near paralysis of mind and action, along with a false sense that everything is just fine. This unfortunate tendency was born out in the summer of 2001: Intelligence sources around the world knew al-Qaeda was up to something massive; there was a frantic sense that an attack was imminent. Did you hear about it? Was the name Osama bin Laden or al-Qaeda on the lips of newscasters? No? How about the names Gary Condit and Chandra Levy?

Historically, our government, no matter which party is in power, has underestimated the ability of the American people to hear the facts, however unpleasant. Traveling across America and speaking to groups of citizens, I have found that when we Americans are informed of the facts we will make the right decision. For example, I found that more than 95 percent of the American people thought similarly to me on the vital issues of preventive law enforcement and swift, sure justice for those who break the law. Our justice system has worked in the opposite direction; in this country, one has a better chance of getting away with a crime than going to jail for it. One report showed only 10 percent of those who commit major crimes get caught, and of that only about 1 percent go to prison. Our lax justice system has turned the saying "Crime doesn't pay" on its head.

These deficiencies in our system weighed in my mind as I surveyed the worldwide spread of terrorism. I knew these problems were connected. The disintegration of our justice and enforcement system was tiptoeing past us, with terrorists following right behind. Sadly, unlike the bear that sleeps through the blizzard and awakes healthy in the spring, we had to go through a devastating loss of life in order to come out of our deep sleep of complacency.

While tracking the Iranian involvement in international terrorism, I began picking up rumblings that the Iranians were looking for someone to jump-start the growth of their cells—someone who could become their surrogate and insulate them from international attention and possible retaliation. I was in contact with the Senate's inner circle during the '80s and was in Washington for many briefings with government leaders, including the president and vice president. A lot of those briefings focused on terrorism and what we could do to stop it. President Reagan had created a White House outreach group to advise on what the public was thinking, and every chance I got, I shared my view that the administration should go public and be honest with the American people on all the facts, even if they were negative, trusting the people to make the right decision. Unfortunately, that's a hard sell to government, no matter which party is in power.

In February 1987, I received a summons from Washington to attend a briefing on up-to-date terrorist intelligence. My son Wayne was in law school at George Washington University and was working at the Justice Department, helping track PLO money. All he was learning pointed to a global expansion of terrorism, with the United States being the final target. I looked forward to our visit.

I had been briefed by my German station chief about further whisperings across Europe that Iran had found someone who fit its needs for the leadership of the international terror army the Iranians hoped to build. "We don't have a name yet," Lemmie said, "but we have a full-court press on to identify who it is and, if possible, neutralize him before he can get operational."

As soon as I instructed my assistant to set up the flight to Washington, D.C., I called a friend in intelligence stationed in Los Angeles, asking about the rumors that Iran had found someone to lead its charge. He said he would set up meetings for me in Washington with people I should meet who would have "things in common" with me.

I was using the funds from the Corporate Security Division to setup the International Intelligence Unit, but it was difficult to get companies to squeeze money from tight budgets for prevention of something that wasn't on the radar screen. My main job was to try and develop a profitable business from all the contacts I was making so we could continue to develop intelligence on terrorism. Every time an attack would occur in Europe or Latin America, the phones would ring for a few weeks with concerns: "What should we do?" The calls would soon fade as the attacks were crowded out of memory by the pressures of life and business. *Anyway,* most thought, *we're in America. It won't happen here. We're surrounded by friends and water. We're immune.* This complacent attitude was prevalent throughout government and business, and all the talking in the world didn't seem to get me anywhere.

Wayne had a condo out near George Washington University, and we made plans to have dinner together. Over the meal, we talked about his work tracking PLO money, and I shared the rumors of a rising terrorist leader. I was also interested in exploring the news that a special young woman had entered Wayne's life, a fellow law student named Althea. (The rumors proved true, and I have a wonderful daughter-in-law and two gorgeous grandchildren to prove it.)

I had briefings the next morning at the White House, so I hugged Wayne, called it an early night, and was in bed by ten.

By nine the next morning I was passing through the Secret Service security check at the White House gate. No matter how many times I go to the White House, even on business, I still get a lump in my throat: "This is the *White House!*" I was walking where Jefferson walked, where Lincoln paced.

Our White House outreach group was put together during the Reagan years. Part of its purpose was to provide feedback to the administration on what we were hearing from average citizens on issues that affected their lives. The main topic of most of the briefings was terrorism. One particular concern was the danger that terrorists and drug lords were joining forces. There was a feeling of urgency as we followed the increase in cooperation between the Latin drug cartels and terror groups that went along with an increase in terrorist attacks. We also were worried by the appearance of automatic assault weapons in our inner cities, particularly the Soviet weapon of choice, the AK-47.

A Name Surfaces

Near the end of the day, I was talking to one of the experts tracking the Middle Eastern terror groups. "What about the rumor there's a rising leader for Iran's international terror network?" I asked. "Yeah, we finally have a name," he said. "Ever hear of Osama bin Laden?" The mysterious son of a Saudi billionaire had been in Afghanistan fighting the Soviet occupation. Bin Laden had all the attributes of a terror leader: charisma, connections, cash, and a killer's heart. He had a growing hatred for Jews and Americans. In fact, his one driving ambition was to drive all the "infidels" out of Muslim countries and establish a true radical Islamic government anywhere he could. Furthermore, he was coming to define as a "Muslim country" any country with Muslims in it. Now it all began to make sense. The question in our minds had been, "If the terrorism was just about carving a Palestinian homeland out of Israel, why were there all these terror groups from around the world being trained in Lebanon?" Not only were they being trained and encouraged to commit terrorist attacks in their own countries; they were linking with the international terror network.

Back at the hotel, I called Lemmie in Germany, waking him from his early morning sleep. "We have a name to go with the rumor," I said. "Osama bin Laden. Can you start gathering all the information you can?" "Sure," Lemmie replied. "Can I finish sleeping first?"

Over the coming months and years, the background and activities of bin Laden rose closer to the surface. Osama bin Laden was not a product of poverty or neglect, nor did he grow up in a bitter refugee camp. He was born in Riyadh, Saudi Arabia, in 1957, one of fifty-four children of construction titan Mohammed bin Laden. Even with all his siblings, young Osama was not neglected but was given the full benefits of a life of luxury. He was known as a pious teenager, well read in Islamic literature, and a regular at mosque services. He graduated from Abdul Aziz University in Jeddah around 1979.

Shortly after his graduation, the Soviet Union invaded Afghanistan to oust Hafizullah Amin and to prop up an illegitimate communist regime. Afghan guerrillas made a desperate plea for assistance from their Islamic brethren, and bin Laden responded. He considered this a higher calling than his father's construction business in Saudi Arabia. While in Afghanistan, bin Laden assisted the Islamic *mujahideen* (literally, "those who struggle for Islam") in their fight against the Soviet army. From December 1979 until the last Soviet tank left Afghanistan in 1991, bin Laden assisted, supported, and fought side-by-side with Islamic *mujahideen* not only from Afghanistan but also from Algeria, Egypt, Sudan, Saudi Arabia, Jordan, Pakistan, the Philippines, and elsewhere.

The Afghan Jihad, as it would be known, was not only a watershed event in bin Laden's life but also a singular historic event that inspired *mujahideen* from almost every country in the world with a Muslim population. For the first time in the modern era, Islamic fighters repelled and defeated one of the world's superpowers. This gave them supreme confidence that they could also successfully defeat the United States. Their success and bin Laden's role caught the eye of the Iranian terror machine. Research revealed that Iran had been active in developing leaders for its worldwide expansion of terror cells. The Iranians had been working for years, infiltrating the countries of the world with their violent Islamic view of the world. Actively recruiting supporters in the Middle Eastern countries, they were always on the lookout for a capable zealot who could advance their worldwide cause. Osama bin Laden, after his testing and preparation in Afghanistan, was a perfect candidate.

In essence, al-Qaeda was born from the aftermath of the Afghan Jihad, when thousands of non-Afghan *mujahideen* left Afghanistan and returned to their home countries, armed with invaluable combat experience against a first-rate military, plus the extensive ties and connections they made in the brotherhood of combat. We also should mention that not all the *mujahideen* returned to their own countries. Many came to the United States. Intelligence estimated that as many as two hundred *mujahideen* moved into the New York area alone at the end of the war with the Soviets.

Birth of Al-Qaeda

AL-QAEDA WAS FORMED in 1990. Its name gives some hint of its function; in Arabic it means "base." It was to be a base, a support, for connected but semiautonomous terrorist groups. Slowly and carefully, Osama took the network Iran had built and started molding it into a cohesive group of committed terrorists who would strike on his command. To most of us, ten years is a long time. To dedicated terrorists it's a twinkling of the eye; they're patient adversaries, and 9/11 was well worth the wait for them. In their minds, they have all eternity ahead of them as they are going about Allah's business, and neither their lives nor anyone else's matter in the scheme of eternity. Failing to understand this fact about our enemies would be our Achilles' heel.

Recruiting for Terror

Bin Laden brought many capable senior leaders and experienced terrorist operatives into al-Qaeda. In fact, he used the strategic alliance business model that became popular among corporations in the '90s. Using this model, businesses formed loose alliances based on common goals, pooling resources for some of their operations. Examples include several car dealerships forming an "auto park" or cigarette companies forming Tobacco Institute. How ironic that a man with such a hatred for the West would adopt a Western business model, except the "businesses" he brought into strategic alliance included Egypt's al-Jihad and Gama'at Islamiyya terrorists groups; the Armed Islamic Group (GIA) and Salafist Group for Call and Combat from Algeria; Abu Sayyaf from the Philippines; Lebanon's Hezbollah; elements of Jamiat al-Fugra, Jamiat Tabliq, and Jamaat al Islami from Pakistan; and Jemaah Islamie, based in Malaysia, Indonesia, and Singapore.

Bin Laden is called emir or prince by his followers. Maybe he should be called the chairman of the board. Al-Qaeda is run like a big business; it has a consultative council staffed by top lieutenants. There are also divisions dealing with training, security, intelligence, and finances. But instead of seeking profits, bin Laden and al-Qaeda seek the removal of all U.S. and Western influences from all Muslim countries, as well as the destruction of the United States and Israel.

An Ominous Goal

Bin Laden's original goal was to radicalize existing Islamic groups, promote his form of Sunni extremism, and support Islamic extremist fighters in Afghanistan, Algeria, Bosnia, Chechnya, Eritrea, Pakistan, Somalia, Tajikistan, Uzbekistan, Yemen, and the Philippines. But that goal has expanded dramatically. Hear this well: Bin Laden now believes in the creation of the *khalifah*—a single, global Islamic state operating under strict *shariah*, or Islamic law. Think of Afghanistan under the Taliban on a worldwide scale. This means that if I don't agree with the extremists' religious persuasion, they have the right to remove me with violence.

Bin Laden developed a business plan early on. The first goal of his plan called for the takeover of Saudi Arabia, using the oil kingdom as the base for his Islamic revolution. The second phase was to move throughout the Middle East and then on to the Far

East, with the United States being the last victim. Al-Qaeda knew that the biggest threat to its success would be the United States and was trying not to do anything too big too soon so as not to invite a massive response. After the anemic response by the United States to the first World Trade Center bombing, the attack on the USS *Cole,* and the twin embassy bombings in Africa, Osama bin Laden was convinced the 9/11 attack would evoke a similar, weak reaction. He didn't expect the twin towers to fall, the American people to become enraged, or the president of the United States to declare open season on terrorists and the nations that harbor them. But terrorists had awakened the American spirit. When our backs are to the wall, we forget about political parties and go after those who attack us.

Part of al-Qaeda's strategy was to try and isolate us from the Middle East, particularly Israel. Al-Qaeda wants us to retreat to our borders and let it work unabated in the Middle East toward the extermination of Israel. Bin Laden and his advisers aren't good students of history, for many powerful countries and mighty kings have tried to bring down the Jewish people and their governments over the centuries. But with the help of a powerful God who created heaven and earth, the enemies were always overcome. Bin Laden, Iran, and all the terrorist groups of the modern world will achieve no different result.

But this doesn't mean we don't face potentially terrible times ahead. I was at a concert recently with a friend whose worldview leans far to the left. He was adamant that President George W. Bush is evil and didn't want him to be reelected in 2004. My friend has versed himself on many issues and is well read. He asked me these questions: "Isn't this war really about oil? If we were to withdraw from the Middle East, replace our dependence on oil with alternative means, wouldn't this stop the killing? Wouldn't we be left alone?"

My answer is "No! No! and No!" Stop and think about this dangerous and absurd theory that many Americans have been brainwashed into believing. First, the notion of *khalifah* and *shariah* predates the discovery of oil in the Arabian desert. Second, hatred for Jews and the dream of their extermination far predates the gasoline engine. Israel offered the Palestinians peace and a homeland and got only a monstrous series of suicide bombings for its trouble, so why should we expect any different? Third, if we stop buying Middle Eastern oil, sending the oil king-doms' economies into the dumps, does that increase or decrease the likelihood of instability in the region and our being seen as the one to blame? Fourth, al-Qaeda and associated terror groups operate across the full expanse of the globe: in oil-rich nations and oil-poor nations, Muslim nations and non-Muslim nations, poor nations and rich nations, secular nations and not-so-secular nations. Thinking the violence will stop if the United States goes home is an America-centric view of the issue. It says our actions are generating the violent reactions when in fact the violence is part of our adversaries' plan of action for reaching their ultimate goal.

Finally, and I believe most crucially, my friend's question places petroleum, not evil, at the core of terrorism. Rather than seeing terrorism as stemming from the darker angels of our nature, to paraphrase Lincoln, it dismisses terror as a matter of politics. Perhaps it's helpful to recall that we are known to our enemy as the Great Satan, not the Great Oil Thief.

An Apocalyptic Scenario

With the United States as the protector both of Israel and the world's flow of oil, we would come to the region's aid with the might of the most powerful military on earth. As the terrorists

know they must destroy preventive law enforcement in a country before terrorism can flourish, they also know they must
remove the United States from any role in the Middle East.

However, the actions going on right now were foretold centuries ago, and the reason I don't believe panic or alarm is called
for is because I have read the Bible, the record left by God himself, and I know what the end will be: Good triumphs over evil.
The end of the book of Revelation makes this clear. Jesus said,
"Be courageous! I have conquered the world" (John 16:33).
Stoking public fear is not godly, for God did not give us a spirit
of fear.

However, this is not to say there isn't going to be a fight that
could get harrowing. The war on terrorism has many fronts. We
are experiencing only the initial skirmishes as the terrorists try to
move on with their plan. Here's a question I have posed to many
knowledgeable people: "What do you think it would take for us
to withdraw from the Middle East and leave Israel to defend
itself?" Let me suggest one scenario.

The technology of the twenty-first century has evolved to the
point that destructive devices the size of a briefcase can kill tens
of thousands, maybe hundreds of thousands, of people in a
crowded American inner city. The question is: Do the terrorists
have such capability? There has been much speculation the past
few years about the 120 missing briefcase dirty bombs from the
old Soviet Union. Well, let's put this to rest: They aren't missing—they're sitting on the open market, available to the highest
bidder.

Recently, I was on the trail of a group stealing passports and
selling them to anyone who had the money to pay. Many individuals from the former Eastern bloc as well as Middle Eastern
terrorists were gobbling up the passports and moving freely
around the world. The trail took me to Vienna where a Russian

informant and I discussed the situation since the collapse of the Soviet Union.

Eventually I asked about the missing briefcase bombs. Her answer stunned me. "Do you want one?" She said it as casually as if she were offering me a ticket to the Vienna Opera. "I thought they were under Russian control," I stammered. "That is the myth of the politicians," she said, "their spin." I could hardly believe someone so lovely could be telling me something so horrific.

She continued to tell me that getting hold of a dirty bomb was a two-step process: The first step requires $50,000, which would get the buyer contact with a man in Moscow. If the buyer is approved, he could purchase the bomb for an additional $1 million. At least, that was the current market price. She told me there was talk of the price going up, due to the demands of al-Qaeda and others wanting to get their hands on the bombs. Forget what spin masters and political opportunists say. We should not be naive about the availability of weapons of mass destruction.

Let's imagine al-Qaeda antes up for a cart full of briefcase nukes. One day, the president is told terrorists have placed dirty bombs in New York; Washington, D.C.; Chicago; San Francisco; and Los Angeles. Their demand: "Get out of the Middle East or we will set off these bombs in your cities." The response will depend on who's in the White House. George W. Bush would likely say, "No blackmail." Suppose then they set one off and then make public their demand. What would the American people do? It might take two or three cities being struck, but at some point our politicians would be forced to withdraw. Then events would begin propelling us toward Armageddon, or something that looks a lot like it.

Considering this possibility and preparing for such should not scare us or cause us to live in fear, especially if we have a personal relationship with the God who created us. Remember, knowledge is power, and knowing the purpose of our enemies can give us the ability to stand as citizens and direct our government to make the right decisions about our future. Sitting on the sidelines as most of us have done is no longer an option. For the sake of our very existence, we must move from the foxholes to the front lines, armed with knowledge, truth, and justice. Western civilization must borrow the mantra of the civil rights movement: We shall overcome.

Osama bin Laden chose to turn his blessings into a curse, his faith into a weapon of fear. We, too, have a choice: to be cowed by that fear or stand in its face, condemn it, and crush it with the weapon of hope.

Hope, however, can do only so much if there are holes in our defenses. We have seen in this book the growth and origin of modern terrorism, the rise of Osama bin Laden, and my experiences in opposing terrorism. But my story has not yet reached the turn of the millennium; the New York skyline is still intact. As my story moves forward, bin Laden is in place, his boldness is growing, and he's searching for a manner in which to strike the United States. He's looking for a weakness in U.S. security that will allow a massive and dramatic attack.

He found it.

Airport Security

TO SET THE STAGE for why al-Qaeda was able to find and exploit a weakness in our national transportation system, I have to backtrack a bit from the days of my pursuit of a beautiful Iranian terrorist operative and my budding international network of intelligence gatherers and law enforcement personnel. In fact, I need to go back to the very first days of my private investigation practice. Imagine a small office overlooking a huge warehouse floor stacked with boxes and pallets, with forklifts and trucks moving in and out all day. Pretty glamorous, right? But that's where I was when I started investigating the trail of unfortunate events that would help make possible the disaster of 9/11.

1974: Introduction to Absurdity

I was sitting at that desk on a sweet spring morning when I received a call from an airline based at Los Angeles International Airport. The fact that I had been called by this international airline was no small miracle, given I had an unlisted phone number and no advertising—not the way one normally builds a business. In fact, God was working on me and my pride, but that's another story. The call from the airline came on a referral from an attorney and client I had met through my church. I was young and green, especially when it came to corporate security. Even my law enforcement experience didn't provide a lot of training that could really help me solve corporate security problems. So as I talked to the airline vice president, I was very vague, using phrases like "There are some methods we use that we just can't talk about." This was private-eye-speak for "I haven't a clue, but I'll make some calls to find out." Fortunately, he was the type of client who didn't ask a lot of questions and took for granted that I knew what I was doing.

The airline vice president (I'll call him Robert Hicks) told me his airline had received an anonymous letter detailing problems with baggage theft and rumors of drug use among its workforce. Hicks knew about the internal problems, but the letter was naming names. "We'll use the letter as an investigative tool," I said, "but don't assume everything in the letter is true. Writers of these types of letters often have an ax to grind." My first lesson as a young investigator was never assume anything. No matter what I was told, I had to check and verify it myself. How many times has a client told me, "Don't worry about Bob. He's been with me twenty years," only to discover that Bob's been helping himself to the office kitty?

The next morning I was rolling down the 405 freeway heading for a 10:00 a.m. appointment at the airline's LAX office. This was my first trip to the airport as a private investigator. It would not be my last.

Arriving a few minutes early, I went straight to Hicks's office and reviewed the terminal layout, other information, and the anonymous letter. As we toured the ramp and baggage areas, I was introduced as a safety expert from Washington sent by the home office to perform a safety audit. This seemed to fly with all the workers.

Even in those initial moments, I noticed the lack of security in the baggage areas. I'd like to say this was due to my astute observation skills, but even a third-grader could have seen nobody was minding the candy shop. Cameras and security personnel were nowhere to be seen. The employees seemed to have free rein, and the baggage was being thrown around like sacks of flour. I observed many pockets where employees could conceal themselves with baggage and rifle through passengers' belongings. The workers themselves? They didn't look anything like the guys in airline commercials—more like the thugs from an episode of *Cops*. Many looked as if they had come straight off the street—or from prison—and had the vacant, bloodshot gaze of habitual drug users.

Uncovering the Problem

We concluded the tour. Swallowing my urge to shout, "Gee, Bob, no wonder you have problems!" I proposed an investigative strategy. I recommended we embed at least two undercover agents with the work crew: one on the day shift and one at night. Additional agents could be moved in, depending on what we uncovered.

The undercover agent is one of the most effective ways to investigate crime in the workplace. Undercover agents must go through the same hiring procedure as real employees, are paid the same, and have to follow the same rules. We try to minimize the number of people at the target company who know about the use of undercover agents; ideally, no more than two will be aware when the strategy is in use. We set up cover billing so the accounting or payroll department would not see a check going to a detective agency. In this case, Hicks and I discussed who would get the reports and be the daily contact for our control agent. I also gathered all the information I could about his airline's hiring procedure so we could brief our agents on how to succeed in the interview process.

I returned to my North Hollywood office, shaken by what I had just learned. Having been in the Air Force and around expensive equipment—and having more than an ounce of common sense—I expected airline security to be very tight and the background checks on employees to be thorough. Could I have been more wrong?

My first task was to find the right agents for the job. Of course, I had told Hicks I had the perfect agents right at my fingertips. And true enough, I was letting my fingertips do the walking now. I needed two males who would fit into the workforce, be able to talk "street," and know drug lingo. It took me a couple of days to find the right guys. Wisely, I told the airline it would take about a week to get the agents up to speed. The agents were briefed on the assignment and report procedure. They were to call in a report every day, then mail me the written copy. I set up a phone line with a recorder attached so they could read the report over the phone, allowing us to have the information the very next day.

The airline's human resources person wasn't in on the undercover operation, so our agents had to earn the job on their own. I set up false identities for them, including cover backgrounds with names and phone numbers of employers. I need not have bothered. To my utter amazement, *not one* of the "former employers" was contacted, and I saw *no evidence* the airline did any background work of any kind. It supposedly performed a county criminal records check, but even that is a meaningless exercise if the employee is from another country, state, or even county.

The agents waltzed right through the interviews and were hired to work on the ramp and in the baggage area, right where we wanted them. They were processed for their LAX identification badges, giving them access to the ramp and other restricted areas of the terminal. Again, I was flabbergasted at how quick and easy it was to plant someone with access to the airplanes.

Our agents reported for work, blending in with their unsuspecting colleagues. Within days they were ringing up the hot line with specific security problems and criminal behavior. The first major problem was the workforce itself. The employees were unskilled and often troubled people who brought their own baggage to the job, so to speak. Many were gangbangers who considered the workplace just another location to commit crime. A *turf* war was raging across LAX, as gang members fought for bigger pieces of the airport pie. At stake was control of baggage theft, drug sales, and the movement of drugs, money, and other contraband through the airport.

A second problem was supervision, or lack thereof. The baggage theft epidemic was a no-brainer. The airline had a low-paid, unskilled workforce operating without proper supervision. The night shifts were the worst. Employees were able to steal at will. Theft was so lucrative and easy, gangbangers probably would have been willing to work at LAX for free.

But the lifting of a few bags by common hoods was the least of the airlines' worries. Our investigation revealed that the accusations in the anonymous letter received at the airline were true, and only the tip of the iceberg. The haphazard security approach created a breeding ground for terrorist and criminal organizations to plant their own people as easily as we did. Drug smugglers were the first to infiltrate the airport workforce, finding it easy to get one of their gang members hired on to work around the airplanes coming in from all parts of the world, particularly Latin America. Our undercover agents witnessed firsthand the simplicity of the operation. Take this edited excerpt from an investigator's report:

Agent 1 observed an unidentified male employee enter the baggage compartment of [airline and flight deleted] which had just landed from Colombia. He emerged a moment later with a medium-sized, crimson-colored suitcase. Agent 1 followed the employee as he casually walked across the ramp, through the underground baggage area and took an elevator to the ticket counter level. Agent 2 picked up surveillance at the ticket counter level and observed the employee walking out through the door between the ticket counters and the back offices. Agent 2 now joined by Agent 1, followed the employee as he left the terminal, observed him heading to a vehicle described as a late-model Ford Mustang, California license plate [deleted]. The employee placed the bag in the trunk, entered the driver's seat, started the car, and departed the area.

This was in the middle '70s, long before terrorists discovered they could do the same thing and have operatives who could place weapons or explosives on an aircraft without detection.

In light of September 11, people may be asking, "If the problems were known so long ago, why weren't they fixed?" The answer is complex but can easily be summarized in two phrases: passing the buck and boosting bucks.

'80s and '90s: Passing the Buck

Many large companies consider security an afterthought or something they only need to make a show of. Security doesn't generate profits, so companies will do what they can to minimize their security expense. One would think airlines with tens of thousands of lives at stake at any given moment would be an exception. No such luck. In fact, the airlines have another ready excuse: With overlapping agencies and companies sharing airline and airport security, they can easily pass the buck, saying, "That's someone else's job."

The buck passing and buck chasing increased in the '80s and '90s as competition intensified. Driven by stock prices, airlines had to keep increasing profits. There are two ways to increase profits: increase gross business—in this case, measured by passenger load—or decrease costs. With the continual expansion of the airline industry and new low-fare airlines getting off the ground, it was hard for airlines to keep increasing passenger loads. So they looked for ways to cut costs. Airlines couldn't squeeze much savings out of pilots, flight attendants, or mechanics without running afoul of powerful unions, so they cast their eye toward the bottom of the totem pole, the terminal workers. They looked for ways to contract out for baggage handlers, food services, and aircraft cleaners.

Before long, all the ramp services were contracted to outside companies. Oh, the workers still wore the uniform of the airline so for awhile the traveling public didn't know any change had occurred. Passengers did begin to notice, however, when criminal activity increased—particularly baggage theft. Still, the squeeze on costs and skimping on security continued.

For example, when our agents went on that first assignment in 1974, the background check was very basic, if it happened at all, and the situation only worsened over time. The Federal Aviation Administration, which is responsible for the air travel system, mandated employee background checks, but the rules were open to interpretation and the airlines and contractors would do only the minimum required and sometimes not even that. Why bother? The FAA didn't hold the airlines accountable when they found they were misbehaving. There weren't any teeth to the rules, no penalties for violations. The holes in the system grew bigger, and every time we came back for another undercover assignment, we found even more problems. The contract system only made things worse. The airlines were telling contract service providers, "If you want to keep your contract, we need an X percent reduction in your fee. And if you can't do it, we'll find someone else who can." The contractor had only one basic way to meet the reduced price, and that was to reduce the hourly rate paid to employees. Contractors also found ways to cut corners on the background check costs, which further limited the effectiveness of the security system. Normally, I wouldn't fault any company for outsourcing to cut costs, but in this case I'm talking about national security.

Why no outcry? Over the years our society and government became—and I'd say has become again—complacent about our nation's security vulnerabilities. As stated earlier, we're surrounded by friends and water; prevention has been the cornerstone of our security approach. This was accomplished by a strong intelligence-gathering ability. A terrorist had a hard time making it to our soil with weapons. However, over the past twenty years and particularly during the '90s, we systematically dismantled our ground intelligence-gathering capabilities, despite the fervent cries of those of us in the intelligence community, both in and out of government. At the same time, the airlines were grumbling, "Why do we need tight airport security? We haven't had any problems with our airliners being hijacked." The explosive combination of weak intelligence and lack of airport security was racing toward a horrific and inevitable encounter. Our nation was asleep, and we would not be awakened even by the alarm sounded by intelligence and security specialists. No, we'd be awakened by the sound of our own airplanes slamming into our own landmarks.

1999–2001: Season of Reckoning

In 1999, my phone rang again. A full quarter of a century had passed since my first visit to LAX as a private investigator. So much had changed: I was no longer green; in fact, I was a little closer to gray. The two little boys who tagged along to my North Hollywood office were now running the day-to-day operations of my agency and detective academy. And instead of toiling in obscurity in the back of a storage facility, I was a regular guest on TV and the host of my own radio show. In fact, this call was from a network TV producer, and what he had to say sent chills down my spine. What I am about to report I have never spoken of publicly. However, in light of September 11 and the absolute need for the American people to understand the issues at hand, I am doing so now.

I had just conducted a secret six-month security audit for LAX, and now this producer was telling me he had in his hand a copy of my confidential report. The report had been leaked! The producer wanted my comments on the findings. "No!" I thundered. "This is privileged information, to say nothing of being extremely sensitive." I further insisted he not use my name or company in any way and urged him a second time to reconsider airing the piece. As far as I was concerned, he might as well have sent the report straight to Osama bin Laden.

But who leaked the documents? "What number is on the report?" I asked. Copies had been sent to about a dozen people at the airport, with each numbered and marked "confidential." He said there was no number on the report and claimed it was not marked confidential. I repeated, "This information should not be broadcast to the public!" Ignoring me and the safety of Americans, the network went ahead and ran the report. The report was instantly picked up by other news organizations and ultimately was used by President Bush's Commission on Airport Security. In fact, so much publicity has been given to the report, my vow of confidentiality has been rendered pointless.

So, what was in the report? What information had I uncovered in my airport security audit that was considered so newsworthy a TV producer would ignore my pleas and air my results for all the world—and I do mean "all"—to see?

Airport Audit:
Fact or Fiction?

THE SECURITY AUDITS my agency did in 1999 and 2000 were eye-openers. Yes, a lot had changed in twenty-five years, but those changes didn't include the anemic security at airports. I was slapped in the face with the undeniable fact that the system wasn't going to change without a major disaster to force the airlines and the government to act.

This round of audits started in a meeting with the head of the airport's security committee, who was the local head of one of the foreign carriers at the Bradley International Terminal. We discussed the problems he knew about, and he took me on a tour of the terminal and lower baggage and ramp areas. After the tour, he asked me to put together a proposal to submit to the security committee, which included representatives of international carriers, the FAA, airport police, and airport management. I presented my proposal to the committee and was told, "Leave no stone unturned, Phil. Find all the security breaches at the airport." I think, later on, the airport was sorry about issuing such a mandate because I documented in writing all I found. This put the security people on notice about the problems. Likely more worrisome was the fact that my information created liability for them if the problems weren't addressed and something tragic occurred.

Besides, executive egos don't like hearing that the system they put in place has weaker security than the average flea market.

I selected a team from our staff to do the audit. We obtained the airport IDs needed to enter the secured areas—again, a stupendously easy process. Our people then entered the terminal and observed all functions to establish a protocol for the audit, which was to take several months. A rise in luggage theft and missing bags made baggage the primary concern of the airlines. However, as we checked the baggage system, we found baggage handling was only a fraction of the security problem at the terminal. Also, we were getting buried in the bureaucratic quagmire involving all the different agencies that worked and controlled our nation's airports. I began suspecting the audit was just window dressing to show all the agencies that the airport had done a study.

It became apparent very quickly that the problems had been years in the making and were the result of putting profit before security. Worse, the solutions weren't going to be simple to implement, thanks to the competing groups always finding new ways to pass the buck.

A System Ripe for Disaster

For weeks, we conducted covert surveillance, discovering how the employees were beating the system. Here's an example: Years before, a camera system had been put in place to watch the baggage belts and unloading bays, but some of them hadn't worked for so long no one knew for sure when they went down. Other cameras were so low to the ground that crooks could cover them with paper without even standing on their tiptoes. Since much of the area was out of the view of cameras, employees had their pick of places to pilfer bags without being detected.

For that matter, it had been so long since the cameras had been used to catch anyone that their presence was no longer even a deterrent, thus defeating one of the main reasons for installing them in the first place. The cameras might as well have been Christmas ornaments.

Security was a joke, literally. We constantly overheard employees cackling about the gaps in security and how management was inept at figuring out how they were stealing items and doing drugs. Baggage handling resembled a Keystone Cops comedy. Workers would stack bags so high on the baggage carts and drive so fast they'd often leave trails of bags around the ramp. Further, on a regular basis, they'd stop on the way to the terminal in out-of-view areas where they were free to rifle through bags at their leisure.

We'd only been back on the job a few hours when we saw the same ramp and gate activity first observed twenty-five years before. Normally, bags come off planes on a conveyer belt, so if someone comes out of the plane with a bag and walks away, that is suspicious. At least, it's *supposed* to be suspicious. But on this occasion the agent on duty saw an employee do precisely that, heading into the baggage area. I asked what airline it was and learned it was a Central American airline; the plane had come in from Bogota, Colombia. I didn't need my private investigator's license to figure out what was in the suitcase. The drug cartels had people working for the airlines in Latin America who would put a marked bag in the baggage compartment on the plane. The cartel's man at LAX would be told which airplane and how to recognize the bag. The Samsonite could have "Cocaine" written across it in fluorescent paint, for all it mattered. The cartel's ramp plant would go on the plane and remove the bag, hide it, and either transfer the contents to a bag he had brought or merely take the suitcase straight from the plane and walk directly out through the exit.

We identified the employee and continued to watch him and any others who might be on the take. A few days passed, and again we saw the same employee go to a plane from Latin America and remove a bag. It was like a twenty-five-year-old case of déjà vu. We tailed him as he entered the baggage area and clocked out on a break. He put a jacket on to cover his uniform, strolled through the exit, found his car, and put the bag in his trunk. We documented the action and had tape of the vehicle so we could arrest him later if desired.

The cartels came to depend on this method of smuggling in drugs, and why not? No couriers were getting caught. Furthermore, none of this was any secret to federal law enforcement. In fact, we had plenty of conversations about it. I asked the Drug Enforcement Administration (DEA), "We know it's happening. We know it has a better chance of happening on Latin American airlines. Why isn't there stronger prevention and enforcement?"

"Two reasons, Phil," DEA said. "Lack of manpower and overlapping security responsibility at the airports." The DEA, which had primary responsibility for stopping drug traffic, simply did not have the manpower to stake out those planes and wouldn't normally even open a case without a tip or informant pointing to a specific flight or individual. If the airport had a team like our unit on site all the time, these criminal activities could be stopped and drugs kept off the street. Simple, right? But immediately the whining would start. "Who's going to pay for it?" The airport? The airlines? The local police? DEA? FAA? If the buck had been passed anymore, it would've qualified for frequent flier miles.

Not only did we know all this, not only did the feds know all this, but terrorist groups knew all this. From information gleaned from captured terrorists, we know they researched and tested the system by getting their members hired long before they were—or will be—needed. They also were successful at buying the services of employees already working at the airport, especially given their low wages. Many of the airport workers remained gang members used to breaking the law, eager to make money, and couldn't care less who paid them. They had no concern for their fellow citizens and the fact that helping terrorists could get Americans killed.

Not having a centralized security system created another serious danger. Contractor A would catch employee A committing a crime. Contractor A would fire employee A. However, because there was no communication between any of the contractors and the airport, employee A would go immediately to contractor B and be hired. After a two-day vacation, he'd be back out on the ramp, working the planes and back in business. Crooks and terrorists don't have to be clever if we're being stupid.

Please don't get the impression that LAX was unusual. All of the nation's airports had major security breaches, with the problems stretching from the front door and ticket counter to the back gates and fences. I'm using Bradley International Terminal only as an example. One of the most blatant failures was the ability to walk past the ticket counter and into the back area, take the elevator down to the baggage area, and walk out to the airplanes. When we discovered this easy way to bypass screening devices, employees laughed and said, "Man, this has been going on for years!" The elevators had keypads, but if someone didn't have a code, he simply waited for someone going down and got on with that person. This happened even though the employees had been told—in fact, it was posted on the elevators—"Don't let anyone on who doesn't have a code." Time and time again over the months we were at the airport we tested this breach and *we were never caught.* Not once. This was the route we saw employees repeatedly use to leave with bags from the airplanes. What would stop a terrorist group from putting a briefcase nuclear device or a biological weapon on a plane and have it taken off in Los Angeles? Certainly not the security system we had, and I am not convinced the Band-Aid changes since 9/11 would be able to catch it now.

Remember that we'd already had a horrible example of what happens when baggage security is lax: the destruction of Pan Am Flight 103 over Scotland in 1988. Few people realize Pan Am was given very specific information about the bomb and the way it would get on the airplane. My director in Germany was a captain in GSG9 and was involved in the raid on the German house where terrorists involved in planning the attack were captured. The raid came twenty-four hours too late. One of the terrorists had already slipped away with one of the radio bombs. Through interrogating his captured cohorts, German agents learned the plan and the type of container holding the bomb. They even learned it was going to be placed on a Pan Am flight heading for the United States. Even though they didn't know the exact flight, security checks could have easily been tightened, especially since the airlines knew what type of container to watch for. The Germans notified the American government and Pan Am. However, Pan Am knew that if it or the government put out a public notice, passengers might panic and the airline would have to ground its flights. So the airline decided to do nothing. Pan Am decided the cost to have the security required would be more than it was willing to pay; it would cut into profits. Because Pan Am did not want to pay, hundreds paid with their lives.

They died unnecessarily. Enough was known that had Pan Am followed the security model of Israel's El Al airline, I believe the bomb would have been found.

We can't even call Pan Am's actions a blunder. It was calculation. A study done for the government in the '80s found that because of international treaties limiting liability, it was cheaper for the airlines to lose an airplane full of people than to pay for the security necessary to keep them safe. Believe it or not, the airlines concluded it was cheaper to pay off the victims' families than to protect their loved ones in the first place. This industry mind-set—the pressure to cut costs and compete for lower fares at the expense of security, coupled with the eagerness to pass responsibility to the next guy—led directly to a steady deterioration of airport security. We got away with it for years. But it caught up to us with a vengeance on September 11, 2001.

Post-9/11: Are Things Better?

I'd love to say we've learned our lesson, that the skies are safe. But the blunt fact is we have not learned our lesson. The pressures to cut costs remain. Attempts to shift responsibility continue playing out in the press. Cutbacks of Transportation Security Administration (TSA) luggage screeners are already underway. And, despite the Transportation Safety Act and the federalization of the airport baggage security personnel, a fundamental problem remains in place: The current workforce isn't the right force.

We are fighting terrorism in our backyard, and we must have strong preventive measures on the home front. I differ with many who want to keep the airport security system in the private sector. Don't get me wrong: I'm a big supporter of the private sector. I've been a free-market entrepreneur most of my working life. But airport safety is a national security issue, and we must have a seamless, unified approach to protecting our airways. We must have police professionals at the passenger drop-off, at the passenger screening and gate areas, on the ramp, and at the remote gates that provide access to the nerve center of the airport. Merely putting the passenger screeners under federal control does little to protect vital national security.

The creation of the TSA force was a political response, a cosmetic fix when an extreme makeover is required. The TSA screeners with their crisp uniforms, magic wands, and shoe searches give a false sense of security to the traveling public; the real danger is what goes inside the airplane from the ramp. Has that changed significantly since 9/11? Are we still vulnerable? Are terrorists still probing for our weaknesses? As we have seen earlier in this book, Islamic terrorist groups, from their earliest days in Lebanon, developed a long-term strategy of attack against America. They would identify our weaknesses while we were comfortable and complacent, and then they would strike us at will. Americans must keep up the pressure on our government to reject Band-Aid fixes and embrace a whole new security approach for our nation's airports. Only then will we be able to travel with a real sense of security.

A Personal Reflection on 9/11

FOR YEARS I HAD been living with the sickening inevitability that America was due for a major terrorist attack on its soil. From terror camps in Lebanon to narco-terror activities south of our porous border to Iranian spies in London to lax security at LAX, the signs all pointed toward a pending day of reckoning for our nation. That I was expecting such a day didn't make the actual day any less shocking, unbelievable, surprising, or horrible.

I had just gotten out of the shower at 7:30 a.m. and was pulling on my pants when the phone rang. Picking up the cell, I heard a shrill yell coming from the familiar voice of long-time friend Leslie Ryan. *Oh, dear God. Something dreadful happened at her house,* I remember thinking. I couldn't make out what she was saying. Maybe she was hysterical, maybe the words didn't register. I don't know. But I finally calmed her to the point I could grasp what she was saying. "New York is under attack!" she gasped. "Turn on the TV!"

I grabbed the remote and jabbed the button while still trying to pull more information out of Leslie. "Planes have crashed into the World Trade Center buildings and something has happened in Washington, D.C." The picture came up on the screen and my heart sank. I saw the fabled New York skyline with smoke pouring from the top and sides of the Twin Towers. In the next instant, the network replayed what was to become a constant reminder of the horror of 9/11: jet airliners plowing into the towers. My reaction was as spontaneous as it was contradictory. "It's finally happening. This can't be happening." The scenes played over and over, each a replay of the nightmare I had been envisioning throughout my twenty-five years in counterterrorism. The evil had arrived. "It's finally happening. This can't be happening."

Witnessing the Unthinkable

Instinctively, I knew this was al-Qaeda. The statements made by Islamic terrorists over the years cut through the cries in New York: "We will visit your cities. Your skyscrapers will fall and your financial centers will collapse." They had been patient. They trained, waited, and watched our defenses decline as they rehearsed their dream of our destruction. This was no rehearsal. This was no Hollywood action movie. This was happening. Worse, it was just beginning.

It was as if all life stopped for me that morning. Hopes that this was some bad dream were dashed as events continued to unfold. Footage from Washington showed a flaming hole in the Pentagon. Having been to the Pentagon, I knew the building was much, much larger than it looks on TV. I knew that what looked like a slice of damage was actually a monstrous wound a block long. I prayed for the Defense Department workers, knowing that those who survived would be setting themselves to the task of war.

Reports surfaced of other planes being hijacked (false) and of a fourth plane that had crashed in a field in Pennsylvania. I knew the crash was connected, and given that the plane went into a field rather than into a landmark, I wondered, *Did the passengers do something to bring the plane down?*

All other aircraft were being grounded, normal radio and TV programming ceased, and the nation's commerce quickly slammed to a halt as we grappled with the horrifying fact: "We have been attacked on our own soil. We are at war." This was not supposed to happen to us. We were the saviors of the world, always helping those in need. We were surrounded by friends and water, a long way from the terrorist strongholds. Terror happens "there"—wherever that is. But not here. We really hadn't been that worried about all those radical terrorists roaming the world; we figured they were thousands of miles from our safe, secure borders. America, the naive.

I was mesmerized by the graphic images: the first tower cascading to the ground, unleashing a monstrous cloud of smoke and ash into Lower Manhattan, sending New Yorkers scrambling for their lives; its sister tower soon following suit; the president being told of the attack in front of a bunch of Florida grade-schoolers, showing heart-wrenching restraint in not reacting in a way that would upset the children; new camera angles of the attack continually streaming into the networks, no angle any less horrible; and from the Middle East, raw footage of Palestinians spontaneously taking to the streets in celebration.

The scenes of Palestinians dancing in the streets celebrating the deaths of thousands of my countrymen ripped open the raw scars of my PLO experience. I was thrown back to my early days in Lebanon, flooded with violent memories of what I had seen and learned about Islamic terrorism, then and throughout the following years. And for the first time since Leslie's call, I was truly, fully enraged. *Where was our warning? How can we still have been so exposed after so many years? What in the world have our intelligence agencies been doing?* Sadly, I felt I knew the answer. The previous ten years under President Clinton had seen a systematic dismantling of our ground intelligence capabilities; he had capitulated to the Left's cries for less and less intelligence and preventive law enforcement. The very evil I had been warning of, the exact consequence of decimating our intelligence capabilities, which I had predicted as early as 1980, had now come to pass with a vengeance. The thing that angered me the most was that we had made it so easy.

Warnings from voices like mine had failed to mobilize the public and prod the federal government, in great part because we had not experienced terrorism here. Oh sure, the first WTC bombing had been a terrorist attack, as were the embassy bombings in Africa, but the Clinton administration preferred to consider them crimes, not acts of terror or war. This only emboldened bin Laden. *Now there can be no excuses,* I thought. But even if this were a wake-up call, would we soon hit the snooze button and fall back asleep? We Americans are known for taking a lot, looking the other way, and just being too busy to get involved until our backs are pressed against the wall. Is this the wall? *I hope so,* I prayed. We had to fight our way out or we might well die where we stood. These people meant to kill us. Period.

As the hours of 9/11 ticked by, it became increasingly obvious that the nation was caught unprepared and our government was in disarray, trying to regain its sense of balance. No image reinforced this more than the uncertainty of the president's whereabouts and the scenes of tens of thousands of federal workers flooding on foot out of the nation's Capitol.

Thoughts of Europe went through my mind. Would we respond like many of the countries of the world when terror strikes? Would we react and enact laws with harsh remedies that would slay many of our freedoms? The dilemma for any country is to find a balance between laws to stop the violence by terrorists and not take away all our freedoms. If we overreact with oppressive laws we could create a fate worse than the results of terrorist violence. This had been part of my message to Los Angeles in the early '80s: "Look at the world. Learn from their mistakes and don't take away preventive law enforcement, which helps us stop attacks before they occur."

Sadly, we'd already demonstrated we weren't good at learning from others when we allowed our defenses to be dismantled during the '90s without even a whimper from the public. And as much as I hoped we would learn from past mistakes, I wasn't feeling optimistic. September 11 was an easy day to be pessimistic, and I got into it, good and deep. We humans don't seem to learn from the mistakes of others. We have to see the destruction for ourselves. Even then, our attention span is short and as soon as some time passes, particularly without any more problems that impact us directly, we fall back into our complacency, busy with our own pleasures. History has shown us the next hit will be bigger, proving more costly in lives and to our way of life. I hoped and prayed, as the afternoon headed toward night, that I was wrong.

I remained glued to the TV set. There was no comfort in shouting at the TV screen such phrases as "I tried to warn you!" and "If you had only listened and acted, this could have been avoided!" My cell phone never left my side as I continually dialed contacts in Washington and other intelligence sources around the world to see if any additional attacks had been stopped or appeared to be in the works. At some point in the afternoon, my professional interest turned to pastoral concern. This was not only a national tragedy, but for thousands of people a deeply personal one. My heart ached for the families of those lost, my grief deepened by my frustration over the government's failure to remain vigilant. My heart also soared in awe at the bravery of the

New York City Fire Department. What spirit does God put in a man that he'd charge into a flaming building when every animal instinct screams at him to flee?

As the scale of the sacrifice and heroism of New York's Finest became clearer, we were also starting to glean more information on Flight 93, which had crashed in Pennsylvania. The story emerging from those last, loving, hurried phone calls filled me with unbelievable pride in my fellow citizens. The passengers had learned of the fate of the three other hijacked planes, but rather than allow themselves to become a weapon against their country, these citizen-soldiers made a stand: "We will not allow the White House or Capitol be attacked." America's first response in the face of attack was not to cower, but to take back control of—if not the plane itself—the country's own destiny. America's first counterattack in the war against terrorism was not launched by the military; it didn't come from the White House but rather with Todd Beamer's simple command: "Let's roll."

Has America ever known a more noble moment?

I was comforted, knowing that the last earthly image of those hijackers aboard Flight 93 was of America as it truly is: not meek, not weak, not afraid—instead, an America willing to fight to protect freedom regardless of the odds, its people willing to sacrifice themselves to protect strangers far below on the ground. They saw Americans: proud, bold, courageous, creative; not needing to take their marching orders from cowards hidden in caves; not heeding the call of a false god claiming to offer salvation through causing the suffering of others; ceding their lives in the divine cause of liberty and sacrifice for their fellow man.

As horrible, as indelible, as incredible as the day had been, there was one thought I could hang my hope on: The last thing those hijackers heard was the cry of the American eagle. And it was a cry of victory.

The Day After

I awoke the next morning at 5:30. September 12 is traditionally a big day for me because it's my mother's birthday. I didn't want the events of the previous day to overshadow my thoughts for my mom. I called her first thing to wish her a happy birthday and to make sure she received her favorite red roses. Though it was my mother's birthday, I'd bet I wasn't the only one who called his mother in the wake of 9/11. There are some things only a mom can soothe.

I returned to my post in front of the TV, watching replay after replay of the Twin Towers coming down, sick with the knowledge that it didn't have to happen. As I discussed in the chapter on airport security, there were holes the size of Afghanistan in our nation's airports, and had they been addressed seriously and effectively, I am convinced we could have avoided the hijackers getting access to planes and carting weapons aboard as if they were nothing more than aftershave. Even after my report was leaked to the press, a local reporter went to the airport and was able to gain access to the ramp and aircraft, using the same tactics I'd warned against in my audit. This was *two years* after the study was done. The reason action wasn't taken then was money. Well, we all paid on September 11, 2001, and the families of those killed paid the ultimate price.

As the news reports droned on, I drifted back to that meeting at Los Angeles International Airport, where I presented the audit report to the security committee. I heard again the bickering among federal agencies, airlines, and the airport over which would pay for all the necessary changes. I heard myself argue that the costs were minor compared to the expense of not acting. And then I began second-guessing myself. *Did I do enough? Could I have done more to bring about change?* One of the issues I faced as a professional private investigator leading one of the oldest detective agencies in the country was confidentiality. I was unable to go public without the clients' approval. To do so without approval would be the kiss of death for any agency that wants to have the trust and future business of large clients. The only reason I talked after 9/11 was that someone else had leaked the report to the press; in fact, as I mentioned before, my report's contents had become part of the documentation for the president's committee on airport security. My obligation to silence was lifted, and the public good now came first. Still, on the morning of September 12, I went a full fifteen rounds with myself before accepting that I'd done all I could do. It was meager comfort.

Every Wednesday evening at my home, I host a small group from my church. For an instant I considered canceling the meeting, but just as quickly the inner voice I heed and trust said, *This is the night above all nights when you need to meet and intercede for your nation.* Around seven o'clock, the group began gathering at my home, all of us still shaken. One look at Leslie's stricken face, and I heard again her anguished wail from the previous morning. I'll never forget that sound. The group moved toward the den. These people knew of my experience in the terrorism field, and I could feel them looking to me for answers and comfort. I could provide instruction and insight, but on this night comfort would have to come from God.

We started by watching the news reports of the day's events. Even a day and a half later, we still felt we were in a dream. "This is unreal. The World Trade Center can't really be gone." Even with my knowledge of terrorism and the warnings I had given, I, too, had trouble believing what I was seeing. I could only imagine what fellow Americans, only now being baptized in the fire of terrorism, were going through.

The time came to turn our faces upward. Nothing on earth or heaven is more defiant in the face of evil than the sound of praise. Our voices rang out; tears poured down our cheeks. "Praise, praise your holy name!" Steeled in faith, we felt ready for the fight. We began to fiercely pray for the families of the lost and our nation. We prayed America would heed the spiritual—and literal—call to arms. We agreed, as only praying partners can agree, that this was America's alarm sounding, and if we didn't wake up, greater evil would follow. And we prayed as David prayed, calling on the hand of the Lord to be our shield.

David might as well have been thinking of Uncle Sam when he sang:

> You will not fear the terror of the night,
> the arrow that flies by day,
> the plague that stalks in darkness,
> or the pestilence that ravages at noon. . . .
> Because he is lovingly devoted to Me,
> I will deliver him;
> I will exalt him because he knows My name.
> When he calls out to Me, I will answer him;
> I will be with him in trouble.
> I will rescue him and give him honor.
> I will satisfy him with a long life
> and show him My salvation.
> (Ps. 91:5–6, 14–16)

The small group broke up, dispersing across Los Angeles, committed as individuals and as a team to continue interceding for our nation and our leaders. The military battle had been joined the day before by the likes of Todd Beamer. And today, the spiritual battle was joined by the likes of Leslie Ryan.

The Post-9/11 Era Begins

The impact of 9/11 began sinking into the nation as the first days passed. The estimated death toll, miraculously, seemed to shrink by the hour. How do two of the world's largest buildings explode and collapse on top of one of the world's most populated cities at one of the busiest times of the day and not have the death toll number in the tens of thousands? Preparation on the part of New York City, heroism on the part of its firefighters, police, and civilian population, and what? As a colleague remarked, "Anything under ten thousand is nothing short of a miracle." Still, there was a huge toll, not only in lives but on the economy. The money markets were declining, small business in Middle America was in trouble, and the hotel and airline industries were in shambles. I wondered, *Was all this planned, or was Osama just terribly lucky?* This was such a low-tech operation that it was almost too simple: Sneak operatives into the country, train a few on the basics of flying an airliner, buy tickets, carry box cutters on board as easily as a comb and . . .

The rest was predictable. Would any of us have acted any differently if we had been on one of the first three planes? We would have done what our crews had been taught: Wait it out. We wouldn't have expected such an evil intent on the part of the hijackers. That changed after 9/11. In fact, it changed on 9/11 with Flight 93. Those passengers knew the score and they reacted. Today we are flying with a different brand of American. This has already been seen countless times since, when passengers and attendants quickly handled problems on board. Has our government moved as fast in the way it operates, or is it still politics as usual? That remains to be seen.

As for me, September 11, 2001, changed forever the way I live, work, travel, and even play. I know I'm not alone on that count.

As the weeks after the tragedy unfolded, I made a commitment to those who paid the ultimate sacrifice on September 11, the rescuer heroes and the innocent who happened to be on the wrong plane or in the wrong building. I also made a commitment to the fighting men and women charged with the task of bringing the terrorists to justice. And I made a commitment to my children and grandchildren. I will do all I can to make sure it never happens again. I hope you will join me.

Homeland Security Act

WHILE I WRITE MY THOUGHTS and share some facts about homeland security and the Patriot Act, I am doing one of my favorite things: I'm sitting at the outdoor patio of Tournesol, a Provençal bistro on Ventura Boulevard in Sherman Oaks, California. As I let my mind drift into the mysterious world of the international counterterrorist agent, I can almost imagine myself in Paris or Vienna, looking into the beautiful brown eyes of that elusive Russian spy, Natasha. Yet, as alluring as the image is, I can also see myself in a Tel Aviv café seconds before a suicide bomber strikes. And then the inevitable thought comes: *Could it happen here? How close are we to random suicide bombings or other acts of terror today? Is our government taking effective precautions?*

Homeland security and the Patriot Act have become household words and, thanks to a few naysayers, fear has begun to rise in the minds of millions of Americans—fear not of al-Qaeda but of our own Justice Department. To whom do we listen? Should we heed the radical voices of a few who try to attribute a conspiracy to the current administration, suggesting the attacks on New York and Washington, D.C., were, if not somehow orchestrated by the right wing, at least used by conservatives as an excuse to take over our country? If we listen to these few voices, we would think we have very bad people as our leaders. It's time to set the record straight, to look at the Patriot Act not in fear or with a political lens but with a somber, factual approach to what the law says and what we as citizens can do.

What is there to fear from preventive measures that our law enforcement can use? I'm certain that 9/11 was not a grand plan by George W. Bush or our government to create a reason to go to war or declare martial law. Bush inherited a system gutted by the previous administration. Also adding to the boldness of bin Laden and others was the way President Clinton handled the terrorist attacks during his watch. Clinton and his group called them crimes, rather than terrorist acts, to appease those in the world who were really not our friends but in action show themselves as our enemies.

Plenty of laws on the books already can be used against citizens if we put the wrong people in power, which can happen in many ways. Primarily, this occurs when thinking Americans stay away from the political process—not even taking a few minutes to vote. This must change. People may get sick of hearing me, but I'll say it again: Citizen involvement is a key factor in keeping our nation safe.

Just the Facts

I want to make a factual, unemotional, and nonpolitical case; this issue is not partisan. From twenty-five years of talking to Americans I have found that 95 percent of us think and react the same when it comes to basic issues of security and protecting our families.

On July 16, 2002, President Bush defined the strategy and outlined the battle plan. He stated, "We are a nation at risk to a new and changing threat." The terrorist threat to America takes many forms, has many places to hide, and is often invisible. Yet the need for homeland security is not tied solely to today's threat. The need for homeland security is tied to our vulnerability. Terrorists wish to attack us and exploit our vulnerabilities because of the freedoms and faiths we hold dear. The president went on to say that the national strategy for homeland security was the product of talking to literally thousands of people and elected officials. He stated this as a national strategy not a federal strategy. The strategy seeks to answer four basic questions:

1. What is homeland security and what are its missions?
2. What do we seek to accomplish, and what are the most important goals of homeland security?
3. What is the federal executive branch doing now to accomplish these goals, and what should it do in the future?
4. What should nonfederal government, the private sector, and citizens do to help secure the homeland?

"Our enemy is smart and resolute," said the president. "We are smarter and more resolute." We will prevail against all who believe they can stand in the way of America's commitment to freedom, liberty, and our way of life.

As Franklin Roosevelt said during an earlier national crisis, "The only thing we have to fear is fear itself." And one thing that leads to fear is a lack of knowledge. I believe that if we know the truth, the truth will set us free. Let's explore some truth. Traditionally, when we think of a patriot, we think of an extraordinary citizen giving his all for his country. The fearmongers have taken the term and run it through the mud so it becomes almost offensive. And, admittedly, radical, antigovernment right-wing militia types haven't helped matters much. What then is the Patriot Act of 2001? It could be cited as the act for uniting and strengthening America by providing appropriate tools required to intercept and obstruct terrorism. Many of the provisions of this act were already available to law enforcement. However, the Patriot Act redefines some of those to make them more efficient for the current battle.

The act covers things like enhancing domestic security against terrorism. Does this sound sinister? Establishing a counterterrorism fund, increasing funding for the technical support center at the FBI, and expanding the national electronic crime task-force initiative are also provided for. All this sounds scary, right? Or could these measures be better seen as common-sense preventive procedures that enhance our ability to be safe in our own country? The act also covers things like enhanced surveillance to intercept communications relating to terrorism and authority to share criminal investigative information among different agencies.

It's important to remember that these were some of the failures that led to the 9/11 attack. Why is this important? Remember what I discussed in prior chapters: The only effective way to stop terrorism is to know ahead of time what terrorists are planning and to halt their efforts. The way we do that is by having good intelligence and having the ability to share with each other the sources and information we have. Prior to September 11, law enforcement agencies were sometimes prohibited from sharing with each other. The reasons for not sharing in the past are complex and almost as old as our country's history. Some of these information firewalls resulted from mandates concerning federal agencies such as the FBI being responsible for domestic problems and the CIA handling problems outside our borders. Some of the lack of communication came from agencies' uncertainty about how much they could share; they took the cautious route and shared nothing. Certainly, petty bureaucratic turf protection also played a part. No more, declared the president. The law now is all the agencies cooperate and share information.

Tools for a Safe Homeland

The Patriot Act clarifies the responsibilities of the director of the CIA regarding information collected under the Foreign Intelligence Surveillance Act of 1947. Furthermore, the FBI has been identified as the most logical and best equipped to expand and be the lead agency in domestic terrorism. The act then brings together the domestic and foreign intelligence-gathering organizations on matters of terrorism and national security. It also establishes training regarding identification and use of foreign intelligence. These steps are crucial if we ever hope to stop future attacks before they occur.

The act also covers international money laundering and enhanced measures to prohibit terrorist financing. Do we want terrorists to be able to easily move their money so they can pay for an attack on us? I suspect some of those attacking the act are using offshore movement of money to avoid American taxes, and some of the teeth in the Patriot Act will make it harder for them to hide their money. My contacts and experiences in Geneva, Switzerland, with private banking there have shown how Americans are still using the foreign banking system to hide their assets from the tax collector. Even though we have laws to allow access to such banking records by American law enforcement, there are many loopholes. The act also deals with international cooperation in investigations of money laundering and terrorist financing. It's hard for me to understand how these measures will be harmful to the large majority of law-abiding, honest, and hard-working Americans.

To protect our borders, both north and south, the act provides for an increase in personnel, better efforts at uncovering criminal backgrounds of visa applicants, and the creation of a foreign student monitoring program. This is particularly important because some of the 9/11 terrorists and others who want to destroy our way of life have come into this country on student visas. The act also deals with humanitarian relief for certain surviving spouses and children, provides aid to families of public safety officers, and expedites payment for public safety officers involved in the prevention, investigation, rescue, or recovery efforts related to a terrorist attack. It also provides for the attorney general and secretary of state to pay rewards to combat terrorism. These seem like good ideas to me.

The Patriot Act strengthens criminal laws against terrorism, with sections on harboring terrorists, providing material support for terrorists, and defining the federal crime of terrorism. It also attempts to improve intelligence, the very area under fire from all sides since September 11. Amazingly, some Americans decry the failure of intelligence prior to September 11 and at the same time condemn efforts to correct the mistakes that lead to the failures. For those sincerely worried about the impact of the new measures on privacy, the act covers protection for citizens and limitations on how law enforcement agencies use the new tools.

Instead of fearing this preventive tool, let's embrace the benefits and make sure we stay involved in our electoral process so we can ensure that reckless, ignorant, or even evil men and women aren't elected to public office.

A Dangerous New World

Let me say it again: There is no going back to the pre-9/11 way of thinking. This event changed all of our futures and left us at a crossroads. Will we take the correct road and stop this evil? Or will we allow it to continue dragging us, like a runaway locomotive, toward destruction?

I believe this evil called terrorism can propel us toward Armageddon. Unlike any other development in modern times, terrorism has the ability to divide the world. We all are aware the Middle East is perhaps the most explosive region in the world, and we in the United States hold the balance that keeps at bay the forces aligned against Israel.

Terrorist groups have had an operational plan and objective for generations, and it doesn't involve peaceful coexistence with the nation of Israel. It doesn't even involve violent coexistence with Israel. It involves *obliterating* Israel, period. There is no concession from this position, only temporary tactical movement. So the first thing we must do is throw out the assumption that if we just give the terrorists what they want, they will stop their violence. No way! The terrorists' evil plan was hatched in Iran, and the only outcome they will accept is a world under a radical Islamic government.

A danger we face now is giving too much credence to the voices that would deceive us about homeland security and the Patriot Act. If we are whipped into a fearful frenzy and fall prey to their propaganda, we will be part of the problem not part of the solution. If we gut these laws, we are back to the naked exposure of the '90s that led to 9/11. It was the lack of a homeland security posture that helped and encouraged the terrorists to believe they could get away with an attack. Our intelligence indicates al-Qaeda is deterred to some degree by tighter security and shows of strength.

Prevention and preparation is the message I have been hammering home to government and corporate clients for the past thirty years. I know from my security consulting experience that companies with no security consciousness or purposeful communication nearly always exhibit more internal problems than companies with good, consistent security policies in place. The same holds for a country. If we don't pay attention to security and prevention our enemies will take that as a sign of disinterest and lack of commitment to react, should they attack. A big part of having a safe environment to live and work in is preparing for the worst and expecting the best. Some of the voices that seek to destroy our ability to have strong preventive tools for law enforcement are just plain naive. They live in a world clouded by a lack of understanding of the evil force present in this world.

Think about it: God himself instructed the children of Israel to send spies to gather intelligence before they moved into the Promised Land. They needed to know what they were facing so they could be prepared. Now, if the God who knows and created everything told his people to go spy out the land, I think it's fair to assume that God wants us to use the intelligence he has given us to help ourselves. And the wisdom of intelligence gathering isn't found only in the Bible; you can also see the same message in Sun-Tzu's *Art of War.* He promotes intelligence gathering as necessary if you want to win your war.

No Bargains with Darkness

Many people live with the mistaken philosophy that if we negotiate with, capitulate to, or appease everyone who opposes us, somehow these opponents will like us and let us have our nice, easy life of American luxury. Wrong. This philosophy has produced an enormous loss of life over the centuries. Hitler slaughtered millions of Jews while the world looked on. Hitler rose to power while good people did nothing but appease him, assuming all would be well. Surely we can't afford to ignore such a horrific lesson from history.

Why is there such an assault on preventive law enforcement measures? The terrorists and those who want an Islamic world government know that they must destroy our homeland security and the Patriot Act to have a chance of succeeding with their insidious plot. The terrorists learned this basic rule in Terrorist Training 101: What is the most effective way to attack our preventive measures? By encouraging Americans—some of them well meaning—to take the misguided approach of appeasement. Our enemy wants us to fight among ourselves.

Many of us are so focused on divisive party politics and posturing that we lose sight of the truth. Or we listen too uncritically to the media. I'm reminded of a former intelligence analyst at the Pentagon who said of the *Washington Post,* "I know how factually wrong they are on matters I know about. I have to assume they're also wrong on things I don't know about." (In fact, she says the only thing she can believe in the *Washington Post* is the box scores for the Redskins games.)

The attempt by the tools of the Left to gut the Homeland Security and Patriot acts can be compared to the situation we found ourselves in in the early '80s, with the attempt to destroy the intelligence-gathering unit at the Los Angeles Police Department. The same kind of preventive law enforcement measures were under attack then. I witnessed the benefit of citizens getting involved after they were told the facts, rather than a political viewpoint. We mobilized thousands of concerned citizens who exercised their right to become involved in running the local government. We stopped the radicals who were the mouthpieces for the terrorists, we kept the LAPD's intelligence-gathering ability, and as a result we had an unbelievably safe 1984 Summer Olympics. Contrast that result to the '90s and the movement during the Clinton years to destroy our ability to find out what the terrorists were planning.

In that case, the voices from the Left won. We dismantled our abilities, and we suffered the consequences on September 11, 2001. I rest my case. I could talk for days and write hundreds of pages to support the need for the Homeland Security and Patriot acts. Remember we do not have to fear the Patriot Act. If we as citizen board members of this big company America do our job and elect righteous and moral men and women, we will not have to fear these laws will be used against us.

But the New York skyline speaks louder than I can.

Lessons from the Past

WHAT SHOULD BE OUR priorities for the future? There is a strong consensus that protecting our people from terrorist attacks of potentially catastrophic proportions is among the highest. This accords with the constitutional mandate of preserving and protecting the nation as the primary function of the government. Remember that in some European countries during the '70s and '80s, the public fell asleep at the wheel and allowed left-leaning politicians to destroy their homeland security measures. Press reports from countries across Europe revealed the avalanche of terror attacks brought economies to a standstill; it wasn't even safe for citizens to shop. Such dire circumstances finally forced the people to rise up and throw out of office those who had sold them out for a misinformed political viewpoint.

In Germany, it took the massacre of the Israeli athletes at the 1972 Munich Olympic Games to wake up the nation. Germans realized they had a broken security system and decided to fix it. They developed GSG9 as the lead agency for their homeland security; they empowered this agency with all the abilities of the different branches of their military and police agencies. But the biggest step they took was to eliminate turf wars between branches of the military and police agencies by placing a military officer in charge of GSG9, a leader who reported directly to the chief executive of the country. Within one hour of an event involving German citizens, GSG9 can have a team airborne. As described in an earlier chapter, Germany's elite team can have the problem solved and be back home before U.S. politicians have finished talking. This must become the model in our country if we intend to be taken seriously by terrorists.

Further, there is the more complex question of priorities within the U.S. homeland security agenda. By establishing the homeland security procedure, these priorities were carefully considered and four areas were identified for extra attention and spending.

1. The need to support first responders is the highest priority at all levels—community, state, and federal.

2. Defending against biological terrorism, along with other weapons of mass destruction, is a concern. A small amount of material capable of killing hundreds of thousands could be used to blackmail us into withdrawing from the Middle East, bringing about the battle that could inflame our world beyond recovery.

3. Border security is a priority because our borders are like a sieve. I have mixed emotions about letting people into our country. Most of us, or our forebears, came here from another part of the world to find religious, political, or economic freedom. We built a country on the principle that under God all people are created equal and have the right to the pursuit of liberty and a just life. I am concerned if our borders become so closed we don't give opportunities to those who seek such a life. At the same time, I am aware that we need strong measures to keep out those who mean to use our freedom of opportunity against us. Many of us will not always agree on every aspect of immigration policy.

4. The government also identifies the need for more information on immigrants, gathered by technology and human assets. Remember the results of not enough human intelligence before 9/11.

As I support the need for a comprehensive homeland security system and investigative tools, my investigation into this area has left me alarmed. Each passing week leaves me wondering if we can be as effective as possible and ready to prevent another 9/11. Our government *is* attempting to react to the effects of September 11, 2001, but is the FBI, the lead agency assigned to the task, prepared? We aren't dealing with a criminal investigation in a local area but a national security problem with the need for fast movement of international information and responses. We were caught asleep at the wheel once, and the enemy is already among us and poised to strike again. I am not concerned about the commitment of top officials such as our attorney general or Homeland Security secretary, and I realize the FBI's good-faith efforts; at the moment the FBI is the only logical choice to lead the effort. However, I am concerned about the lack of experience of front-line supervisors and field agents.

Admittedly, the FBI is the world's premier law enforcement agency. It is the best at solving crime and has the most advanced technical support services anywhere. However, some attributes that make the FBI number one in crime solving become a negative in fighting terrorism. One of those weaknesses is the decentralization of its structure. As an example, the FBI will work a regional crime but not share information with other regional offices or FBI headquarters. In crime solving this works well but becomes a problem in the fight to stop terrorism. Another weakness is the lack of experience in world terrorism on the part of line supervisors and field agents. International terrorism has not been the priority of the bureau, and many field supervisors have only a few years with the bureau. As mentioned above, another concern is the timeliness with which information gets reported to other regions. Some of the deficiencies are known and are being addressed. The problem is that the bureau and other federal agencies have operated the same way for years; getting them to change is like trying to turn an aircraft carrier with a canoe paddle.

I believe our president and those responsible for homeland security understand these problems, but I'm not sure if they understand the urgent need for immediate change. A situation that occurred at the Los Angeles airport between Christmas and New Year's Day 2003 tells it all.

A Fright on the Town

The nation was at code orange, high alert, around the holidays. There was specific and credible evidence that al-Qaeda was planning an attack on the United States involving international flights. One airport mentioned was Los Angeles International. I had to go to LAX during this time to pick up a friend. Evidence of tightened security was everywhere. Usually drivers can approach the airport by a handful of routes; however, that night the street approach to LAX was confined to Century Boulevard for passenger cars and Sepulveda for limousines, buses, and taxis. I was in a limousine with no license plates—only a small window sticker on the right bottom of the front windshield identified the vehicle. As we came off Sepulveda to the airport entrance, we encountered a traffic block; officers were checking all vehicles entering. To my surprise, when we approached, one of the security agents merely waved us through. We kept going. A short distance ahead was another checkpoint where police were searching all cars. But as we approached an open lane, again—to my dismay—we were waved through. We hardly slowed. I still can't imagine why that happened. We were driving with no plates to identify the car. The windows were tinted so checkpoint guards had no way of even seeing what we looked like. We could have easily been loaded with explosives and slammed right into the front of a terminal packed with holiday travelers. This was an abysmal security breach when our nation was at its second highest level of alert and had evidence specifically listing LAX as a potential target. Understandably, when I related this security lapse to various government officials responsible for airport security and counterterrorism, they were aghast.

I believe one of the reasons for these kinds of security breaches is the lack of a cohesive, seamless security system directed by professional police officials. Security agents manning the checkpoints appeared to be private security guards who obviously were untrained and unprepared to think as security professionals. I can only imagine all the similar breaches across the country—lapses made even more ominous by the fact that we were on a high security alert. When we analyze information about terrorist operational procedures, particularly al-Qaeda's, we see that terrorists do extensive preoperational surveillance and trial runs to test security systems. Over the holidays they were watching, evaluating how we performed, and looking for holes such as the one my limo rolled through. Al-Qaeda and other terrorist groups are watching to see how seriously we take the threat to our homeland. We are viewed by the Islamic extremists as soft, self-centered, morally bankrupt, and easily distracted. Frankly, when the biggest story on Monday after the Super Bowl of 2004 is not the specific warnings about al-Qaeda's planned use of an aircraft over the weekend to deliver a biological weapon but, rather, Janet Jackson's right breast, one has to believe they have a point.

As the president states repeatedly, we are in danger of dropping our guard because we have not experienced another attack since 9/11. Yes, we have made inroads against al-Qaeda. We have buried or captured many of the top leaders, including the number-two man, but they and their cohorts are still in high gear. Think about their ability to conduct multiple, nearly simultaneous attacks against several targets worldwide, such as in Turkey and Morocco, even after the downfall of many al-Qaeda leaders. The manner in which these attacks are conducted indicates refined capability and sophisticated tactics.

There are those among us who would like us to believe that the worst is over, that we should reduce our preventive measures by doing such things as gut the Patriot Act, limit the Homeland Security Agency, and give little heed to our open borders. Do our successes against al-Qaeda and other international terrorist organizations give us reason to back off and return to our pre-9/11 habits? Available intelligence tells a different story; it reveals a new generation of terrorists around the globe, with footprints leading to Pakistan and Iran. In the recent proliferation of terror, from Turkey to Bali, two striking trends are clear.

First, global terror is no longer in the hands of the "centralized" system of Osama bin Laden's al-Qaeda. The new wave is characterized by a different, more local dynamic. Second, most of the terrorist outfits spanning the globe have a Pakistani connection, using the backbone of that country's *jihad* factory: the mosque network, the *hawala* network, and Pakistan's own all-powerful, all-pervasive military-intelligence complex (particularly the Inter-Services Intelligence organization), which provides terrorists with weapons, training, and infrastructure. Even though the Pakistan government is helping us in the war on terror, a great many in the military and intelligence service support the radical Islamic approach and the Taliban. Moreover, Pakistan's Lashkar-e-Taiba Islamic extremist group is fast becoming the global successor to al-Qaeda. This evil we call terrorism has many heads. If we cut off one, another takes its place.

A December report that was released to the public, the president, and Congress by the advisory panel to assess domestic terrorism response capabilities raised some of the same concerns I raised earlier. One concern, mentioned above, is doubt about whether the FBI can be structured to effectively lead the fight against terrorism in the homeland. One of the areas the panel noted was intelligence sharing. According to the report, too little information is shared with state and local officials, despite improvements in ways the government handles such information. The Rand survey, commissioned by the advisory panel on terrorism and later declassified, found that only about half of local law enforcement agencies and half of state and local emergency management organizations have received guidance from the FBI about the type of terrorist activity information they should collect and pass on to the FBI. The Gilmore Commission recommends that to improve intelligence sharing, the president should:

- Designate a federal authority that can speed up the granting of security clearances for state, local, and private officials.
- Provide training to allow these officials to use intelligence information.
- Overhaul the current classification system to improve the dissemination of critical intelligence.

I think the U.S. government must seriously consider establishing the equivalent of England's domestic intelligence organization, MI5. This agency would be dedicated to preventing terrorist attacks and coordinating international intelligence with the CIA. The main difference from the FBI would be that the new organization would be staffed by intelligence professionals. This would leave the FBI free to do what it does best: fight and solve domestic crimes. If we aren't careful, we will dilute the effectiveness of the FBI in crime solving by changing its focus to national security issues. Also, a separate organization, out from under the umbrella of the Justice Department, would diffuse some of the frenzy around the attorney general. We must act now and not wait for another 9/11.

For us as American citizens, the question is, will we, the people, rise to the occasion? Furthermore, the question is not, will our government do what is right to protect us? We have a choice, and the future of our children—indeed, the very existence of our way of life—is at stake. The war on terror will not be won by governments; it must be waged and won by individuals. We each can make a difference and cut through the shackles of terrorism threatening to enslave us.

The Israeli Factor

AS A YOUNG CHILD growing up in the Bible Belt of the Midwest I was taught that we were to love and support the nation of Israel and the Jewish people. My parents would share the rich stories of how the Jewish people were God's chosen race and that the Messiah had come to the world through the Israelites. I could picture the young Jewish boy in Nazareth learning the carpentry trade at Joseph's side, then traveling the dusty roads up to the temple on feet that would one day walk on the Sea of Galilee. As a teenager, I'd sit in the Grand Theater in Chillicothe, Missouri, getting lost in biblical-era epics like *The Ten Commandments, Ben Hur,* and *The Robe,* imagining myself crossing the Red Sea with Egyptian troops at my back or sitting with the multitudes as Jesus preached his Sermon on the Mount. Although I hadn't been to Israel and had little understanding of its customs or way of life, I reached adulthood feeling very close and connected to its people. I knew this corner of the world had been very special in God's plan and was set to play an important role in his return. And I ached to travel to the Middle East and experience firsthand the land where Jesus walked.

My lifelong dream of going to the Holy Land was fulfilled in the spring of 1977, when I joined a tour organized by High Adventure Ministries. The trip was meant in part as a show of support for Israel and the Jewish people. Ministry founder and friend George Otis, who would later build radio and TV stations in southern Lebanon, believed this was his mission, and I eagerly accepted his offer to go with him.

Our group of fifty shared the same section of the plane for the long flight to Israel. We were no stoic and sedate church group; we had the enthusiasm of college students heading to spring break in Cancun—though our behavior wasn't quite as rowdy. As our plane made the descent into the Tel Aviv Airport, we broke into a praise song, our hands raised in the air. I will never forget the feeling as the wheels touched down on Israeli soil. We were still rolling at about a hundred miles per hour, but already I sensed this was a homecoming. I heard the words of the prophet Micah: "Come, let us go up to the mountain of the LORD, to the house of the God of Jacob. He will teach us about His ways so we may walk in His paths" (4:2a). Already I felt a racing in my spirit, telling me this path would fundamentally change my life. Certainly that has been true, though if I had known how "high" some of the adventure would be I might have run the other way. Then again, maybe not. In his book *Wild at Heart,* John Eldredge argued that if we are honest with ourselves, there are only three desires of a man's heart: We long for a battle to fight, an adventure to live, and a beauty to save. I was at the start of my battle and adventure.

I remember as if it were yesterday my first day waking up on Israeli soil. The early morning breeze and the smell of the Mediterranean Sea gently urged me to consciousness. Sticking my head out the window, I was immediately struck by how clean and fruitful Israel appeared. I could feel the vitality and excitement of life on the street below and the vistas beyond. Somehow it seemed at once new and vibrant, and ancient and timeless, like the frontier days of our own country, I imagined.

As I traveled the country with my tourmates, I was taken with the lush green countryside, the groves of fruit trees, and the healthy-looking people of the nation. I'd been in Israel only days and already I was in love. Here was the beauty I hoped to save.

As enchanted as I was by such surroundings, I was taken aback by the drive into the Arab sectors. The closest thing I can compare it to is crossing the border from San Diego to Tijuana, Mexico. One minute in paradise and the next in abject poverty. I remember being conflicted about this contrast, and I wanted to find the reasons for it. Immediately I began to hear it was Israel's doing. That was the Arab view and the media view. Then, digging deeper, I learned firsthand all the things the Jewish people were doing to help their neighbors raise their standard of living; I saw no such effort on the part of nearby Arab nations. Nor was there any recognition of the Israeli effort on the part of the Western or Arab press. The difference between my media-formed assumptions and my on-the-ground experiences was startling. Earlier in this book, I talked about the things I witnessed at Israel's northern front, where the press misrepresented the truth or else actually staged false stories. This marked the beginning of my education on the antics and antagonism of the Western media. A quarter century later, I can testify that little has changed in that regard. And certainly, not much has changed in the Arab sectors—despite the size of the late Yasser Arafat's personal bank accounts, I might add. There is poverty where there could be plenty, anger where there could be education, violence where there could be vibrancy. And there is an indisputable and despicable effort to blast Israel out of existence.

Some Americans wish us to abandon Israel. Some wish us to force Israel into making massive concessions to the Palestinians for a separate homeland while Palestinian leaders tell their supporters Israel will be pushed into the sea. These critics of Israel want to redraw the map of the Middle East. (By the way, many Arab maps still don't show Israel, even after fifty-five years.)

Other Americans look at all the tax money heading toward Israel, the Palestinians, and more moderate Arab neighbors; they see the violence and say, "A plague on both their houses. Forget choosing sides. Choose America!" They want us to withdraw and keep our money at home.

The Case for Supporting Israel

I approach the question of supporting Israel as I do an investigation case. I consider the assignment and determine a strategy. The goal is to determine if we have justification to support Israel against its Arab neighbors (not counting the two that have already made peace with Israel). Does this question have two sides, and would it be reasonable for us to take the side of Israel? Or should we push Israel to compromise at any cost, including the matter of who controls Jerusalem? One of the things my agency does at a strategy meeting is to determine the investigative techniques we need to use: background, research, interviewing witnesses, field work, and so forth.

We've already seen some of my field work results, the reports I read from the terror training camp, and, additionally, the time I spent on the ground in Israel, meeting with military and political leaders. I was learning the players and the true story and experiencing the wrong end of missiles and machine-gun fire. But there are eyewitnesses other than myself and people mentioned in this book; we also have the witness of history. And, in any case involving witnesses, we must compare statements for inconsistencies and then compare their statements to their actions.

In this investigation we have a tremendous amount of background information to explore, with plenty of investigative work in research, comparing what we find with other records for verification. A primary—though hardly our only—source for determining a position toward Israel comes from the historical record in the Bible.

Before we go any further, let me admit that the approach I've outlined may put us in difficult waters with some readers and certainly with many in the world. But as a professional investigator, I'm used to reluctant clients. In many cases over the past thirty years, the clients really didn't believe the facts when presented; they had a conclusion in mind coming in, and no matter how thick our file of contradictory evidence, they wouldn't budge. I know with this topic that many won't believe our findings, no matter how compelling the facts. But instead of giving up and saying, "What's the use?" we must approach the investigation with even greater commitment and diligence.

So let's move ahead. And it seems that the first topic we have to deal with is the issue of the land, the Promised Land.

The Biblical Background

This story starts in Genesis 12:1–3 when Abram is told by God, "Go out from your land, your relatives, and your father's house to the land that I will show you. I will make you into a great nation, I will bless you, I will make your name great, and you will be a blessing. I will bless those who bless you, I will curse those who treat you with contempt, and all the peoples on earth will be blessed through you." When I first discovered this promise from God, I thought, *Yes, I want to be blessed! Who doesn't?* So right off the bat we find a pretty good reason to support Israel: If we bless and support God's chosen race, we can expect favor and blessing in return.

As soon as Abraham entered the land, the promise concerning the land was made more direct: "I give this land to your offspring, from the brook of Egypt to the Euphrates River"

(Gen. 15:18b). Later, God told Abraham, "I am God Almighty. Live in my presence and be devout. I will keep My covenant between Me and you. And to you and your offspring after you I will give the land where you are residing—all the land of Canaan—as an eternal possession, and I will be their God." A biblical covenant was more than a mere contract that could be rewritten, renegotiated, or exploited for loopholes. A covenant was very serious business; a formal, solemn contractual bonding that meant serious problems for any king or party that chose to break its provisions. Here, God himself was making a covenant with Abraham.

I paraphrased the covenant, which was a package deal that included four basic promises:

1. "I will give you the land as an everlasting possession."
2. "I will greatly increase your numbers, and I will make of you a great nation."
3. "I will make an everlasting covenant to be your God and the God of your descendants."
4. "I will bless those who bless you, and all people on the earth will be blessed through you."

So what are the boundaries of this Promised Land? When we examine the record, there does not appear to be one definitive, fixed description of the boundaries. But in Genesis 26, a very significant statement about the land is made. The Lord appeared to Isaac and said, "Do not go down to Egypt. Live in the land that I tell you about; stay in this land as a foreigner, and I will be with you and bless you. For I will give all these lands to you and your offspring, and I will confirm the oath that I swore to your father Abraham" (vv. 2b–3). Meanwhile, Exodus 23:31 places the boundaries of the Promised Land from the Red Sea to the Mediterranean Sea and from the desert to the Euphrates River. Joshua 1:4 describes the land extending from the desert and

Lebanon to the Euphrates, including the Hittite country, to the Mediterranean on the west. So although it is difficult to precisely reconstruct a map of the Promised Land, we can reasonably conclude that it was the territory formerly occupied by the Canaanites, Amorites, Hittites, Perizzites, Hivites, and Jebusites. I think for our purposes we have factual information that shows the Jews were promised a homeland, generally in the area of current Israel—as opposed to South America or Australia or even more locally in Egypt or Iraq. Do we honor or dishonor this promise? Do we bless or do we curse, and in turn be blessed or cursed? For me the choice is easy. I will take blessing over curses any day.

If we call the original covenant a title deed to the land, there would appear to be little doubt about the divine right of the Jews to possess the land for all time. "I will give the land where you are residing—all the land of Canaan—as an eternal possession" (Gen. 17:8b). I'm reminded of the promotional campaign featuring messages supposedly from God. One reads, "What part of 'thou shall not' don't you understand?" It's tempting to hear God say, "What part of 'everlasting possession' don't you understand?" When we look at this promise in the context of the whole covenant, it seems impossible to separate it from the other three promises. Yet many in the United States who support Israel, including Christians and even some Jews, try to separate the land from the other promises, somehow jumping to the conclusion that if God would have anticipated the volatile situation of 2004, he would say, "Compromise on the land. I really didn't mean for you to have it forever." Putting aside the silly notion that the current situation is a surprise to God, I have another problem with this idea: If we accept that God would break his covenant, then all God's promises could be situational. Christians, do you think the promise of eternal life through Christ comes with an asterisk?

Which brings us to another reason Christians in particular have a very strong reason to support the Jewish people: the love and status God gave them by choosing the Jewish race to bring his salvation into the world. Abraham was the first to get wind that Christ, the Messiah, would come from his seed, and certainly the genealogy that kicks off the Gospel of Matthew lays out Jesus' Jewish line. Read passages such as Genesis 49:10a, which states, "The scepter will not depart from Judah, or the staff from between his feet, until He whose right it is comes." Here we get a glimpse of the expanse of God's vision. God brought the Jewish nation into being as part of his plan to send his Son, the Messiah, as Savior of the world. First, God called Abraham, then he established the nation through Abraham's descendants. Next, God gave the monarchy through the tribe of Judah. In time, Jesus descended from this kingly line.

Where's the connection with terrorism? Go back to Bethlehem, in particular the part of the story that usually gets left out of our Christmas pageants. When Jesus was humbly born in that stable, all hell tried to kill him: the Jewish Messiah, the newborn Jewish king. Instead of suicide bombers, Satan used Herod, who sent soldiers with swords and spears to slaughter all the male infants in Bethlehem. *Jewish* infants. This was terrorism, though in a different form. Can we honestly say we're not fighting the same fight today, particularly in the Middle East? Are the actions of Hamas so different from those of Herod? Every suicide bomb, every shot fired, and every missile launched at a Jewish victim is another attack launched straight at heaven. This is a fight to the finish, and we need to understand the unique role that we, as believers in God and Americans, have in this fight.

America: Israel's Friend or Enemy?

MANY PEOPLE IN THE United States, including some Christians, have tried to make the argument that though the Jews brought the Messiah into the world, because of their actions, they have since used up all their goodwill and should pay for their mistakes. Support for Israel should be withdrawn. Putting aside the obvious anti-Semitic undertones of that argument, the issue for America is not about whether Israel deserves our support. It's about whether Israel *requires* our support as part of our effort to protect ourselves and all freedom-loving people. As we'll see, abandoning Israel would be a fatal mistake for us as a nation.

I am equally alarmed when I hear Christians in America making statements like, "Even if the Bible seems to say that the Jews have divine right to the land for all time, is this the only way to interpret the Bible? Is there only one way of reading the promises about the land and predictions of a return to the land?" Others ask, even more shockingly, "Is there even a direct connection between the children of Israel, the Jewish people, and the state of Israel today?" They seem to think that if we take the Bible at its face value and choose to believe that God keeps his word, we are being one-sided in our political stance, we're being unfair or worse, racist. While accepting or equating two sides of a situation appeals to our sense of fairness—particularly in our world of moral relativism—this is a dangerous viewpoint, particularly if it were to become the policy of our government. Even a small amount of research on the events of the day shows that U.S. support of Israel is crucial to holding off an attack on *us* by Israel's enemies. As I revealed in the chapters dealing with Iran, terror groups, like Hezbollah, already have a presence in this country. The Great Satan mind-set behind the Iranian hostage situation remains. Syria, along with Iran, is behind Lebanese-based attacks on Israel. It was doing its utmost for Saddam during the recent war, including shuttling terrorist fighters into Iraq. Finally and perhaps most obviously, don't the terrorists already link Israel and America? Are we not one in the minds of the terrorists? Osama bin Laden himself is incapable of writing a paragraph that doesn't condemn "the Jews and Crusaders." And remember who was dancing in the streets on 9/11.

If we follow the road of appeasement to the radical Islamic terrorists, we could be directly responsible for a premature rush toward a cataclysmic conflict. Radical Islamic leaders don't want a compromise or to live in peace with Israel. As I write this, today's newspapers describe how Israel released hundreds of prisoners in exchange for the bodies of a few citizens. Their reward for this gesture: a bombing in Jerusalem that murdered ten people.

Yes, occasionally a Palestinian leader will toss out a public statement trumpeted in the media as a "breakthrough," but it soon proves to be nothing more than a tactical response geared to satisfy world opinion or buy time for further armament. Listen the next time a leader of Hamas, Hezbollah, or Syria makes an overture toward Israel. And don't read only the headline; find the whole statement. Wait for whomever said it to further expand on his initial comments. I'll bet the price of this book we will find a list of conditions longer than an ayatollah's beard. By the way, the Middle East Media Research Institute at www.memri.org is a wonderful resource for English translations of articles and speeches by major players in the region.

Christians, the threat to Israel is a threat to you. Look at it this way: The apostle Paul told us that believers of Christ have been grafted onto the branch of the Israelites. If I graft a small branch onto a larger branch, it eventually is hard to tell where the original ends and the grafted branch begins. Their growth and fate are now tied together. If I take an ax to the main branch, the grafted one dies as well. If terrorists are allowed to chop down the Jewish nation, Christians, too, will fall.

It is time to reverse the brainwashing by the world. If this evil of terrorism is really about some miscarriage of justice carried out by the Jewish nation, what is the injustice? What acts of evil has the Jewish nation done to deserve the hell being heaped on its people on an almost daily basis? From the arts to sciences, finances to philanthropy, have not the Jews been a blessing to each nation they've inhabited? It really does seem the only act that has truly infuriated their enemies was their being chosen by God as his people, the Prince of Peace coming into the world through Jewish blood.

Since my first involvement in the region in 1977, I have seen the onslaught against the Jewish people increase to an almost frenzied level. The reason I originally became involved in this fight was to help Christians in southern Lebanon, but my real passion was to stand with Israel and not only pray but work for the peace of Jerusalem. In my spirit I knew it was the right thing to do. Even though we built the Voice of Hope radio station a couple of miles inside Lebanon, we knew in the back of our minds we were helping Israel stop the terrorist missiles raining down on its northern front. At the time my perception of the problem was limited to the turmoil evident within a day's drive of the Arrizme Hotel. It has taken me thirty years of pulling on the thread of terrorism to see its source, reveal its structure, and understand its global dimension. Israel is like a levy built against the flood of terrorism. We can't allow it to break.

Which gets to the next point: I've stated the biblical basis for Israel's right to the land and argued that God's promise can't be changed to fit political niceties. And now I come to the irony: For all the talk of the land, for all the debate about a Palestinian homeland, at the end of the day, Israel's present conflict—and our response to it—has virtually nothing to do with that parcel of turf along the Mediterranean.

Not the Land but the World

I am very concerned when I see and hear Christian writers and leaders trying to rationalize terrorist attacks—including 9/11—as stemming from a miscarriage of justice toward the Palestinians by the Israeli occupation of the West Bank and other areas. Those who try to tie the terrorist attacks of bin Laden and al-Qaeda to a violation of UN resolutions by Israel, the West Bank occupation, and our support of Israel need to reconsider some of the basic facts about international terrorism. Consider the 2003 bombing of a historic synagogue in Tunisia. The message certainly wasn't, "You'll be better off leaving Palestine." The message clearly was, "You Jews are not welcome or safe anywhere." Indeed, persecution and assaults on Jewish interests are on the rise worldwide. Is it protest of occupation or process of elimination?

Even a cursory look at modern terrorism shows it has nothing to do with the Middle East situation, per se, but the broader terrorist goal of changing the world to a global, radical Islamic form of government. Remember, Osama's original goal was to take over Saudi Arabia. How does anger toward the leadership of that kingdom relate to Israel? It doesn't. How is Israel connected to the establishment in the 1970s of international terrorist training camps in Lebanon, whose only goal was to train groups from all over the world to go back and disrupt their own governments in concert with the radical Islamic agenda? Again, look at the headlines: What do blowing up Australian tourists in Bali, French engineers in Pakistan, and UN workers in Iraq and trying to blow up Russian theatergoers have to do with Israel? Even more chilling and recent is the horrible death toll in a Russian school resulting from terrorist occupation.

The death spirit of radical Islamists, born of a demonic desire to destroy all good things of God, wants to consume far more nations than Israel. But let's put aside the spiritual element of the fight against Israel. Instead, let's assume someone finds all this Bible talk a bunch of hogwash and sees the Israel-Palestinian conflict as the political equivalent of two strangers fighting for the same parking space. Why choose one over the other? Or for that matter, why even care if the two destroy each other fighting for the spot? We must care because the Palestinian "car" is packed with explosives and coming straight from a garage filled with similar cars (literally in some cases) heading all over the world. We must care because the terrorists' sources of training and support are international, with international goals. And we choose Israel because the other side has chosen to make war against us.

My first indication that this wasn't about a homeland for the Palestinian people came when I saw the records of terrorists from all over the world being trained in the Lebanese training camps. What was the reason? They weren't there to fight Israel. Why were they needed, since they were sent back to their own countries to be in place for future action? Israel was to be the focus of the most violent attacks but was only the first target. The rest of the world was also in the crosshairs of the terrorist sights, with the United States being the big prize.

I think one of the most succinct summaries of the situation came from a radical Islamic leader's speech in Saudi Arabia. He said, "First we're taking Saturday, then we're taking Sunday." In other words: first the Jews, then the Christians. First Israel, then America.

Many might think I am anti-Muslim or that I am against the Arabs as a people. Nothing could be farther from the truth. It is very important that we in the United States, and particularly those of us who call ourselves Christians, show love for all people, even if we have to condemn acts of violence by members of a certain race or religion. This love shouldn't be at a distance. I have close friends who are Arabs; I developed many loving friendships while in Lebanon. My traveling the world tells me that most of the world's people, if given the chance, are like me and want the same things from life that I do. When I encourage support for Israel, I am not at war with the general Arab population but a few radicals who are misusing the Muslim faith as a tool for evil. I am at war not with people but with the spirit of darkness that brings death instead of life. The devil's hand was as much on the gun that killed Yitzak Rabin as it was on the guns that killed Anwar Sadat.

The Case for Israel: Summary

On the grounds I've listed, my decision to stand with Israel is as easy as it is crucial. My own views have been shaped from my childhood lessons about the role of the Christians in standing with the Jewish people and the importance of the very land where Jesus walked. They're shaped by my many visits to Israel before the visit with Major Haddad that changed my life. They are certainly shaped by my experiences in Lebanon with the Palestinians and in my decades of counterterrorism work since. And my position is shaped by history. Time and time again, we've seen enemies of peace and life try to destroy what God intended for this special piece of ground and the people to whom he promised it. We must not be shocked by current events, nor can we be discouraged. Instead, we must raise the standard and plant our feet firmly in the land.

After concluding that we still have a mandate to stand with and in support of Israel, what do we do? As I've said, the purpose of this book is to empower others by giving them knowledge. Only with knowledge backed by facts can they make the right decisions. Many Christians aren't effective because they aren't prepared to discuss and defend their positions. That is why I keep encouraging people to learn all they can about terrorism and its origins. When speaking with others about the Israeli situation, I present these facts in a way that doesn't force them down the listeners' throats. I have found from my many debates with those on the Left and from countless speeches that when these issues are presented in the right way, most will listen and agree.

God loves all people, including Arabs and all other Muslim people. Support for Israel does not translate into hate or anger toward them. If we are going to make a difference and have our voices heard, we need to speak with authority but at the same time with love. If we hope to promote support for Israel, we have to do it from God's viewpoint and not the world's. Trust me, it is very easy for us in the Christian world to become overwhelmed and intimidated by the power and persuasion of the world's viewpoint. For Americans this can mean falling into the trap of vengeance and discrimination. We can only change if we are emboldened with knowledge and abounding in grace. It is amazing what peace we can have if we are prepared and confident in what we are saying. Remember, Christians aren't responsible for the results, only the presentation.

We are also directed to support, love, and pray for the Jewish people and the nation of Israel. We are told to pray for the peace of Jerusalem and support the efforts to keep the Holy City free of violence, to maintain it as a place where God's people can come to worship him.

I'm reminded again of my first visit to Israel. One day during the trip, I separated myself from my High Adventure companions and wandered to the site where Jesus spoke his Sermon on the Mount. The contours of the terrain form a natural amphitheater, which explains how the Master's words could be heard across the multitudes. The air was still and sweet. The presence of God was palpable. I sat down, looking up the hill to where Jesus stood. Soon I could feel his words floating down to my ears: "'Blessed are the peacemakers, for they will be called sons of God'" (Matt. 5:9).

I thirst to be a peacemaker, to work to stop those who make war on God's chosen people. Will you join me?

In the next chapter I will discuss what the Jewish people are up against and how deep and organized is the hate against this tiny nation. I was surprised to learn of the systematic anti-Jewish doctrine written into the education system of the Palestinian Authority's schools. They want us to believe young children decide on their own to kill themselves, along with innocent people. What evil hides in the hearts of men to destroy the mind of an innocent child? With this information I hope to convince Americans that it is even more important we stand up for Israel. Let's look at the facts.

Children as Weapons

IS THERE HOPE for peace in the Middle East? What is the future for the Jewish people of the region? I think these questions can best be answered by looking at the practices of the Palestinian Authority leadership in training children. Most Americans would find it offensive to think about children being encouraged to kill themselves for a cause. But we must understand what we are facing. We must realize that the entire world doesn't look through our eyes and see things the way we do. Many parts of the world do not value life as we do.

Those of us who have children can remember when our children were two, three, and four; we recall how quickly they learned and retained what they saw and heard. It would be unthinkable for us to consider our own children being deliberately exposed to vivid descriptions of death through pictures, video, books, and even songs. But this is what young Palestinian children are forced to listen to and experience. The trainers at the suicide schools and the Palestinian leaders take great pride in saying that no one is forced to become a suicide bomber and that these "martyrs" are volunteers. But day after day in the schools these impressionable young minds receive systematic indoctrination to hate Jews and Americans. As we are about to see, the curriculum of the Palestinian schools supports hate for those who don't think according to the radical Islamic agenda, pushing aside even those parts of Islam that teach nonviolence. Even the Muslims' own greatest prophet, Muhammad, at times opposed violence and suicide. He forbade "harming innocent bystanders," even in times of war. How do they respond to Sheikh Abdul Aziz bin Abdullah al Sheik, the supreme religious leader of Saudi Arabia, who issued a *fatwa* (religious edict) in April 2004 that equated suicide bombings with suicide, something forbidden in Islam?

Given such Islamic teachings, why does the campaign of suicide and murder continue? It continues, on one hand, because Palestinian leaders have failed to provide hope and opportunity for their people. For the young people of the Gaza Strip, hope consists of marching children masked in *kaffiyehs* and carrying toy guns; hope is pictures of young suicide bombers on every wall, beckoning others to follow. On the other hand, we have seen Yasser Arafat urging them on to become his pride and joy, the next martyrs. Arafat went on to explain that dead Palestinian children—*shahids*—are the greatest message to the world.

The Palestinian Authority has gone all-out to capture the hearts and minds of the young people. Imagine flashy music videos enticing children to be combatants and to aspire to death. I'm not talking about the kind of videos seen late at night on MTV or on cable. I'm talking about videos I have viewed that are marketed to Palestinian kids in the same way Nickelodeon and *Teletubbies* are marketed to American youngsters. They show eleven-year-old Palestinian girls articulating why they want to die for Allah—"Because the afterlife of *shahid* is best." These Palestinian Authority videos instruct children to attack soldiers with stones and attempt to allay their fears. "Don't be afraid," the ten-year-old actor in a popular video repeatedly sings to his five-year-old listener. "The stone in your hand will turn into a rifle." Hitler's propagandists had nothing on Arafat.

We in America don't understand the time or effort leaders such as Arafat put into the preparation of these young suicide bombers. They pour millions upon millions of dollars and years of time into creating an army of misguided, suicidal robots. What might have happened if, over the past twenty years, Arafat and the other leaders had put this much effort into building up the infrastructure in their territory and creating jobs?

Is this an isolated phenomenon, or is it more pervasive? The long-term success of any political solution to the current Palestinian-Israeli conflict will depend on the willingness of all parties to negotiate and abide by mutually agreed conditions. But the Palestinian belief that martyrs can solve problems in this conflict jeopardizes any possibility of a successful political solution. Unfortunately, there is little international recognition of this issue. We hear the myth that these acts of martyrdom result from desperation. This implies that some sort of Marshall Plan and democratization will resolve the problem.

Building a Culture of Hatred

However, this hatred and urging to violence is extremely widespread; it results from a deliberate, carefully planned, well-orchestrated campaign that draws on a strongly held cultural belief system and a variety of deep-seated psychological training modes. These are not acts of desperation; they are the detonation of weapons that have been years in the preparation. The CIA and other intelligence agencies have conducted studies into the PLO education system. Let's look at some of the training methods to produce children as weapons.

Although Palestinian Authority leader Yasser Arafat signed multiple agreements—the Oslo and Wye River accords, for example—to forgo violence and to work for peace, he didn't stray an inch from his decades-long goal. He instigated a program to mold the Palestinian population, from earliest childhood, into this destructive mode of behavior. Recent generations of Palestinians have been absorbing with their earliest memories the notion of reclaiming Palestine "from the Zionist entity" through *jihad*. Martyrdom had not been used for centuries within Islam, but the concept was revived by Ayatollah Khomeini prior to the Iranian revolution and became an increasingly prominent tool in militant Islam since the 1960s. It was adopted by the primary nationalists, the Sunni Muslim Palestinians. Relying on certain interpretations of passages in the Koran, it also resonates with Sunni populations as part of their culture, especially when religious and national leaders advocate it. Palestinian children are urged to violent actions against Israelis even when it is likely they will be injured or die. They are encouraged to desire rather than to fear death because they will find a place in paradise with Allah. They will be revered as heroes in the land of the living because they will have obtained the highest honor in Islamic society.

Mobilizing children to military activity is a widespread phenomenon in much of the Middle East, and it starts as early as the age of seven. As far back as 1982, the Palestinian National Liberation Movement, Fatah, then under the leadership of Yasser Arafat, has been active in Lebanon, drafting children from the age of twelve into active, bloody service, while children from the age of seven played an important part in the Palestinian intifada that started in 1988.

Further, the official textbooks authorized by the Palestinian Authority as well as teachers' training guides for summer camps for kids (essentially military training camps) promote the glory of martyrdom. They've even developed a TV campaign emphasizing the message of violence and indoctrinating children in self-destruction for Palestine and for Allah.

Poisoning the Wells of Knowledge

How did schoolbooks come to be used as tools of hate? In 1948, Egypt and Jordan controlled Gaza and the West Bank, respectively, following the Arab attack on the newly declared state of Israel. The textbooks created for use in these territories were based on those used in Egypt and Jordan, which denied Israel the right of existence and advocated war to "reclaim" the land that had been under Arab rule before the UN partition of Palestine in 1947.

In 1967, during the Six-Day War, Israel overran the West Bank and Gaza and came to administer the disputed territories. The schoolbooks were then reedited by Israeli authorities to remove anti-Israel sentiment and promote the legitimacy of the state of Israel. Even though the textbooks were reprinted, clandestine photocopies of the excised portions were circulated in the schools and oral classroom teaching continued to encompass the hateful material. In many of the Palestinian refugee camps, the old, hate-filled editions were used exclusively.

In 1993, after the signing of the Oslo Accords, the Palestinian Authority under Arafat began to govern Gaza and the West Bank and was mandated to assume control of education. Despite the requirements of the Oslo Accords for peace and reconciliation, the deleted anti-Israel material was immediately reinstated. Not only that, but the Palestinian Authority then published accompanying guidebooks that explicitly directed the teachers regarding specific violent methods, some thirty-one guidebooks in all. The Israeli MGO, a Palestinian media watch group, conducted an extensive analysis of newspapers and TV programs before and during the intifada that started September 2000. The MGO study indicated that the Palestinian Authority TV programming massively escalated its presentation of numerous clips specifically advocating that children should sacrifice their lives for *jihad* and the fight against Israel. Less TV incitement was documented in 1998 by a separate organization, Peace for Generations. It analyzed a *Jihad for Kids* videocassette, in which children recite and sing words like these: "Ask for blood and we will drench you. / When I wander through Jerusalem, I will turn into a warrior who sacrifices himself. / In battle dress, in battle dress, in battle dress . . ." To which their teacher applauds, "Bravo, Bravo, Bravo." Such hatred should give us a new appreciation for Barney.

Continuous monitoring and documentation of Palestinian Authority programs expose what is being devised for the children, even now. One such videocassette, *The Journal of a Child Self-Sacrifice,* was translated into English and annotated by sources, dates of recordings, and newsprint, bearing the logos of the Palestinian TV stations that aired the videos.

Let's look, in the Palestinian Authority's textbooks, at some statements and poems first-graders must learn:

1. "The youth will not tire; they desire to be free or perish. We draw our water from death and will not be as slaves to the enemy." (Palestinian National Education for First Grade, *My Home Land,* 67–68 N.B.)

2. "Know my son, that Palestine is your country that is purest soil red with the blood of martyrs. Why must we fight the Jews and drive them out of our land?" (*Our Arabic Language for Fifth Grade,* 64–66)

3. "Regarding demongration of Jews [racism] mankind has suffered from this evil in both ancient as well as modern times." (*Islamic Education for Eighth Grade*)

These concepts are used not only in civics texts and texts on Islam but in every subject taught, including Arabic language and grammar exercises. Here's an example: "Determine what is the subject, and what is the predicate in the following sentence: 'The Jihad is a religious duty of every Muslim man and every woman.'" (*Our Arabic Language for Fifth Grade,* 167)

Can Americans imagine teaching their elementary-school children these kinds of concepts? My young daughter just entered her teenage years. I can't imagine filling her mind with constant hate and violence and encouraging her to kill herself for an unholy cause. Again, the Palestinian Authority under Arafat signed various agreements to clean up the textbooks, removing all violent and anti-Israel statements. In some cases the Palestinians have made cosmetic changes to comply with the anti-incitement requirements of certain European nations that support the PLO with funding. In most cases, however, they have not made any sort of effort. And even if the textbooks were sanitized, there remain the teaching guides, which simply include for teachers' use the material taken out of the textbooks. Here's a quote from one such teaching guide: "Scientism: The students should conclude the reasons the world hates Jews. The student should explain why the Europeans persecuted the Jews." (*A Report on the Teacher's Guide,* number 022, 7, and corresponding student textbook *The Contemporary History of the Arabs of the World,* grade 12, 151)

In summary, the teaching program conveys that the "Zionists" must be expelled from the land. The Jewish state of Israel is the conqueror, thief, and enemy. Children are taught that Jews want to rule the world; and Palestinians should hate and kill the enemy. "We must take back our land, our Palestine. Jihad is our duty. Death as a martyr is glorious. The martyr will be rewarded in heaven."

The three Rs taught to Palestinian children are rage, resentment, and retribution.

Marketing Death

If only it were just books. As mentioned earlier in this chapter, the Palestinian Authority has also gone high-tech. Ironically, it's using various Western influences—even producing MTV-inspired videos. One such fifteen-minute video includes an original sound track with Arabic dialogue and background music with an overlay of English translations and explanations. The production creates an overall effect of intense drama and emotion. The visual presentation is as important as the spoken messages. They combine to create a powerful emotional effect on its viewers—mostly young people.

Music, with its obvious emotional influences, is a prominent feature of the video. Sometimes with a gripping martial rhythm composed of a repetitive drumbeat, sometimes triumphant, sometimes quiet, plaintive, and nostalgic before rising to a crescendo enhanced by evocative lyrics, the sound track of the video is a masterpiece of emotional manipulation. The chants used in the production are those often heard at funeral processions following Hamas or Islamic Jihad suicide bombers killed in terrorist attacks. Everything is designed to enhance the messages of the narrative: the tears of a bereaved mother, throwing stones at the hated occupiers, going off to be a martyr. Images fade into one another: colorful, intense battle scenes; somber funerals; fantasy images of a future in paradise. Flag-waving young rock throwers are glorified and eulogized; lush roses open and bloom as the message plays: "How sweet is the fragrance of the earth, its thirst quenched by the blood flowing from the bodies of youthful champions."

The message is a directive for children to embrace violence and to desire martyrdom. Each clip illustrates a separate theme, and the narrative is supported by accompanying visual images.

Children are prominently portrayed as fighters, as young heroes. What child doesn't want to be a hero?

I've observed examples of some of these clips. My descriptions follow:

- Palestinian Authority TV, recorded May 2, 2001: The narrator tells seven- and eight-year-old children that the time for toys and games is over. "Throw away your toys and pick up rocks." The clip then shows this happening.

- Palestinian Authority TV, recorded January 11, 2001: A young boy is shown talking to an even younger child. The shot dissolves from one child to another, shaded in beautiful gold and orange colors. The older child reassures the younger about throwing stones at armed soldiers. "Don't be afraid," we hear his plaintive voice singing in the background. "Don't be afraid, Allah is with him. A stone in his hands has turned into a rifle. Don't be afraid."

- Palestinian Authority TV, recorded July/August 1998: To the background of music and lyrics referring to suicide bombers, we see scenes of training in a summer camp for children. We see parades of boys and girls in uniform. They perform gymnastics and training exercises and jump through hoops of fire. The older boys and girls assemble machine guns. Younger ones, appearing to be eight to ten years old, are standing at attention as a coach recites. They repeat what he says: "Children of my country, I am a suicide squad . . . As long as the mine explodes . . . Allah is the greatest . . . I return to my country . . . The blood of the land of Jerusalem . . ." It has been estimated that nearly fifty thousand children were enrolled in such military-style camps.

I can give other illustrations, but more aren't needed. Such training and indoctrination aren't limited to the Palestinian-controlled territories. Wahabi-funded schools, even on our own soil, carry out such teachings. The point is clear, frightening, and disheartening: One of the biggest battles in the war on terrorism is going to be for the minds of the children.

If we listen to the news reports or have heard comments by Arafat, his successors or apologists, it appears they are seeking peace with Israel and want only reasonable accommodation. We have been told by the Arab press and liberals in this country that Arafat was not a terrorist and that he was moderate. Yet, after Oslo 1993, the picture changed dramatically—once Arafat had full control over the Palestinian territories. The Palestinian Authority went into high gear, openly inciting hatred in the schools, in the mosques, on TV programs, in books, in newsgroups, and in military camps, all the while giving even more emphasis to the virtues of martyrdom. Arafat said in January 2002 on Palestinian Authority TV of a child grasping a stone and facing a tank, "Is it not the greatest message to the world when that hero becomes a martyr and dies for Allah? We are proud of them." On August 18, 2002, Palestinian Authority TV aired a memorial for a fourteen-year-old girl who died in conflict. In the program, Arafat exhorted children, "onward together to Jerusalem," to which the audience gave a programmed response, cheering and chanting.

Many sources report that hordes of young men clamor to be sent to their own obliteration. Hamas and Islamic Jihad established a selection process based in mosques; a zealous youth ready for martyrdom gets noticed by clerics who recommend him for selection. Thereafter, the selected one enters a proactive, highly supervised, and disciplined regimen of spiritual studies and paramilitary training. The individual is taught to see suicide operations as a way to open the door to paradise for himself and his family.

The Palestinian suicide bombers are willingly available in a never-ending stream. A Palestinian psychologist, Dr. Massalha, who studied Palestinian children ages six to eleven, reported that more than 50 percent dreamed of becoming suicide bombers. What is a more hellish idea than that of children wanting to grow up and kill themselves?

Massive indoctrination of children and young adults has been immensely successful in helping to generate this abundance of suicide bombers. The passion for a violent end is not an emotion of reluctant resignation in the face of oppression; it is motivated by eagerness, even joy, at the prospect of self-annihilation and the murder of the enemy. "To life," say the Israelis. "To death!" answer the Palestinian children.

Can the societal influences, indoctrination programs, and their long-term outcomes be reversed in the Palestinian children of the future? A developing child is influenced by many factors: genetic, constitutional, mode of child rearing, and belief systems of the parents and their societies. We in Western societies must understand that this phenomenon will not go away overnight; only with changes in the education process, curriculum, and teachers will we see a positive, nurturing environment develop.

Effects on Palestinian Children?

The current conflict and cultural mind-set has significantly affected the mental health of Palestinian children. Dr. Massalha's research indicates that one in every three Palestinian children suffers from psycho-social problems. In the northern part of the Gaza Strip, 73 percent of six- to eleven-year-olds suffer from post-traumatic stress disorder (PTSD), of which 39 percent are moderately to severely affected.

PTSD, at its worst, causes severe emotional and mood problems; it can incapacitate its victims socially, academically, and behaviorally. Traumatic experiences lead to increased neuroticism, high-risk behavior, and low self-esteem, all factors that can contribute to self-destructive behavior.

The Gaza community mental health program has been particularly active, reporting an increase of at least 30 percent in children needing help, and this is without any sort of adequate screening program in the schools. The Palestinian minister of education recommends that schools offer the children time for written and oral expressions about the situation and ask them to draw pictures. However, teachers are not trained to conduct such activities. Even though international donors have given financial support for locally based mental health programs, the funds have not been used—at least not for their intended purpose. Clearly, the urgent need for screening, diagnosis, and mental health management for Palestinians has been ignored.

In our society, when a single child is abused, the media call it an outrage. When a dozen children are abused, the media call it a scandal. When a whole population of children is abused and molded into murderers, the media call it . . . well, they don't call it anything, do they?

Frequently, I hear the question: "Is there hope for peace in the Middle East?" Resolving Middle East tensions and stopping worldwide terrorism are both crucial to achieving world peace. Terrorism as we know it today springs from the terrorism factories of the Middle East. Hezbollah—supported by Iran—Hamas, and other forerunners of al-Qaeda gained their birth and training in the common battle to push Israel into the sea.

If the Palestinians should ever denounce violence against Israel, the outlook for their children, who for decades have been programmed for violence, is better. However, unless something is done to change the mind-set not only of the current generation of Palestinians but for future generations, the videos will play, the evil creeds will be imprinted on malleable young brains, gruesome death will be exalted over a productive life, and the blood of Abraham's children will continue soaking the soil.

The Solution: The Power of One

FOR ME, AND I HOPE for others, this is not the end of the story but the beginning. Now others have the benefit of the knowledge I've gathered on terrorism, its origin, and its evil intent. Before we look at solutions and actions needed to win this battle, I pose two questions:

1. Can we afford to lose the war on terrorism?
2. What does losing really mean?

As an investigator I'm not offering a politically flavored viewpoint but, rather, what I believe the facts point out. We have had many presidents from both parties make tough decisions on military matters: President Roosevelt (World War II), President Truman (Korean War), President Kennedy (Bay of Pigs), President Johnson (Vietnam), and President Clinton (strikes on Bosnia in 1995 and on Iraq in 1998). There were eight presidents—five Republicans and four Democrats—during the Cold War that lasted from 1945 to 1991. I don't intend this to be a political statement, and those who take it as such miss the truth.

Our country is now facing the most serious threat to its existence since World War II. The deadly seriousness is greatly compounded by the fact that very few of us think we could actually lose this war and even fewer realize what losing really means.

When Did the Threat Begin?

Many will say September 11, 2001, was the start of our problems. The answer, as far as the United States is concerned, is actually 1979, twenty-two years before September 2001, with the following attacks: U.S. embassy hostages in Iran (1979), Lebanese embassy and marine barracks in Beirut (1983), Pan Am flight to New York destroyed over Lockerbie, Scotland (1988), first New York World Trade Center attack (1993), attack on the Khobar Towers Military complex in Dhahran, Saudi Arabia (1996), U.S. Embassies in Kenya and Tanzania (1998), and the USS *Cole* (2000). Keep in mind the facts in chapter 5 about the true origin of terrorism; during the period from 1981 to 2001 there were 7,581 terrorist attacks worldwide. The threat really began long before.

Why were we attacked? Could it be for envy of our position, success, and freedoms? The attacks happened during the administrations of Presidents Carter, Reagan, George Bush Sr., Clinton, and our current president, George W. Bush. We cannot fault either the Republicans or Democrats because there were no provocations by any of the presidents or the immediate predecessor, President Ford.

Who were the attackers? In each case, the attacks on the United States were carried out by Muslim extremists.

The World's Muslim Population

Muslims make up about 25 percent of the world's people. Isn't the Muslim religion peaceful? Hopefully, but that is really not material.

There is no doubt that the predominately Christian population of Germany was peaceful, but under the dictatorial leadership of Hitler (who was also "Christian"), that made no difference. The people either went along with the fanatical leaders or they were eliminated. The Nazis killed 5 to 6 million Christians for political reasons (including seven thousand Polish priests; see http://www.nazis.testimony.co.uk/7-a.htm). Thus, almost the same number of Christians as Jews were killed by the Nazis, yet we most often hear of atrocities against the Jews. Although Hitler focused on the Jews, he had no hesitancy about killing anyone else who got in his way—be they German Christian or other nationalities.

The same evil intent guides the Muslim terrorists. They focus attention on the United States, but readily kill anyone in their way: their own people, the Spanish, the French, or anyone else.

The point is that just as the peaceful Germans were no guarantee of protection to anyone, neither are the peaceful Muslims a protection for us from the terrorist Muslim leaders and what they are fanatically bent on doing.

There is no way we can honestly say that our enemies are anyone other than the Muslim terrorists. Trying to be politically correct to avoid verbalizing this conclusion could well be fatal. There is no way to win if we don't clearly recognize and name the enemy.

If we are to win, we must clearly answer the two pivotal questions I posed at the beginning of the chapter.

We can definitely lose this war, and, as odd as it may sound, the major reason we can lose is because many of us simply do not fathom the answer to the second question: What does losing mean? A great many of us think losing the war means hanging our heads, bringing the troops home, and going on about our business, as we did after Vietnam. This is as far from the truth as we can get.

If we lose this war, we will no longer be the premier country in the world. The attacks will not subside but rather will steadily increase. Remember, the terrorists want us dead not just quiet. If they had only wanted us quiet, they would not have produced an increasing series of attacks against us over the past eighteen years. The plan was clearly to stay on the attack until we were neutralized and submissive.

We would, of course, have no future support from other nations, for fear of reprisals. Furthermore, they would see we are impotent and of no further use to them.

Having subdued the United States, the terrorists would then pick off other non-Muslim nations, one at a time. It will be increasingly easier for them; they already hold Spain hostage. It doesn't matter whether it was right or wrong for Spain to withdraw its troops from Iraq. The Spanish did it because the Muslim terrorists bombed their trains and told them to withdraw the troops. Anything else they want Spain to do will be done. Spain is finished.

The next will probably be France. Our one hope for France is that the French might see the light and realize that if we don't win, they are finished too; they can't resist Muslim terrorists without us. However, it may already be too late for France. France is already 20 percent Muslim and fading fast.

If we lose the war, our production, income, exports, and way of life all will vanish. After our losing, who would trade or deal with us if they thought it would incur the terrorists' wrath? If we can't stop the terrorists, how could anyone else? They fully know what is riding on this war and therefore are completely committed to winning at any cost.

Until we recognize the costs of losing this war, we cannot unite and put 100 percent of our thoughts and efforts into winning. And make no mistake—it will take a 100-percent effort to win.

So, how can we lose the war? Again, the answer is simple. We can lose the war by imploding: defeating ourselves by refusing to recognize the enemy and its purpose and failing to dig in and lend full support to the war effort. If we are united, there is no way we can lose. If we continue to be divided, there is no way we can win.

Let me give a few examples of how we simply don't comprehend the life-and-death seriousness of this situation.

Norman Mineta, President Bush's secretary of transportation, refused to allow profiling, though all of the terrorist attacks were committed by Muslim men between seventeen and forty years of age. Does that sound as if we are taking this thing seriously? This is war; for the duration, we're going to have to give up some of the civil rights we've become accustomed to. We had better be prepared to lose some of our civil rights temporarily, or we will most certainly lose all of them permanently. Some might argue that this is a slippery slope, but remember we gave up plenty of civil rights during World War II but immediately restored them after the victory and, in fact, added many more since then. Do I blame President Bush or President Clinton before him? No, I blame us for blithely assuming we can maintain all of our political correctness and all of our civil rights during this conflict and have a clean, lawful, honorable war. None of those words apply to war. Americans should get those words out of their heads. Remember, as voters, we are board members of this great company, America. We need to be active, vocal board members.

Some have gone so far in their criticism of the war or the administration that it almost seems they would like to see us lose. I hasten to add that this isn't because they are disloyal; it's because they don't recognize what losing means. Nevertheless, such conduct gives the impression to the enemy that we are divided and weakening. Furthermore, it concerns our friends and does great damage to our cause.

The recent uproar, fueled by politicians and media, regarding the treatment of some Muslim prisoners of war by a small group of our military police perhaps exemplifies best what I am saying. Remember, these prisoners are from a group (the Iraqi military) that only a few months ago was throwing Iraqis off buildings, cutting off their hands, cutting out their tongues, and murdering them for disagreeing with Saddam Hussein. Only a few years ago, the Iraqi military chemically poisoned four hundred thousand citizens of Iraq for the same reason. The prisoners also represent the same enemy who recently burned Americans and dragged their charred corpses through the streets of Iraq. And still more recently, this same enemy was providing videos of the beheading of an American prisoner to international news sources. I am not saying that the U.S. military members who broke the law should go unpunished.

But compare this with some of our press and politicians who for several days thought and talked about nothing else but the "humiliation" of some Muslim prisoners—not burning them, not dragging their charred corpses through the streets, not beheading them, but "humiliating" them. The politicians and pundits have even talked of the impeachment of the secretary of defense. I submit that all the focus by the press ensures more beheadings of Americans. When we compare the press coverage of the American being taken hostage and beheaded, one has to wonder who our press is supporting. What is their agenda? Are they so hateful at President Bush that they are willing to encourage more violence against Americans?

If this doesn't show the complete lack of comprehension and understanding of the seriousness of the enemy we are fighting, the life and death struggle we are in, and the disastrous results of losing this war, nothing can. To bring our country to a virtual political standstill over this prisoner issue makes us look like

Nero playing his fiddle as Rome burned: totally oblivious to what is going on in the real world. Neither we nor any other country can survive such internal strife. Again I say this does not mean that our politicians or media people are disloyal; it simply means that they are absolutely oblivious to the magnitude of the situation the Muslim terrorists have been pushing us into for many years. Remember, the Muslim terrorists' stated goal is to kill all infidels. That translates into all non-Muslims, not only in the United States but throughout the world. We are the last bastion of defense.

Our nation has been criticized for many years as being arrogant. That charge is valid in at least one respect: We believe we are so good, powerful, and smart that we can win the hearts and minds of all those who attack us. With little effort, we can defeat anything bad in the world. I'm sorry to have to be the one to break this news, but we can't. If we don't recognize this, our nation will not survive, and no other free country in the world will survive if we are defeated. Name any Muslim country in the world that allows freedom of speech, freedom of thought, freedom of religion, freedom of the press, or equal rights for women.

If we don't win this war right now, keep a close eye on how the Muslims take over France in the next five years or less. They will continue to increase the Muslim population of France and continue to encroach little by little on the established French traditions. The French will be fighting among themselves over what should or should not be done, which will continue to weaken them and keep them from any united resolve. Doesn't that sound eerily familiar?

Democracies don't often have their freedoms taken away from them by some external military force. Instead, they give their freedoms away, politically correct piece by politically correct piece. And they are giving those freedoms away to those who have shown, worldwide, that they abhor freedom and will not allow it to anyone or even to their own kind, once they are in power. They have universally shown that when they have taken over they start brutally killing each other in a contest to decide who will be the few to control the masses.

We all know the power of unity, whether in a business, a family, or a country. Our survival as a country will be secured only if we join together. Let's look at what we have learned on this journey to unmask terrorism and use this knowledge to inspire us to unity.

First, we have discovered that terrorism wasn't created by an oppressed people being brutalized by callous persons in power. Nor was it created by misguided students aiming to overthrow a dictator. Nor was it created by people who had their homeland denied to them. Terrorism at its most basic is the use or threat of violence to inflict fear on innocent people in an effort to control or corrupt them. And the source of this destructive spirit lies at the core of the human problem of evil.

The evil of terrorism is deeper than any simple power struggle or political agenda, and we must apply appropriate solutions. As I've stated before, I am a vocal supporter of preventive law enforcement as a front line against terrorism. I understand that the only effective way to deal with terrorism is to prevent it. But I have come to realize that the kind of prevention I've learned from more than thirty-five years in law enforcement won't be enough to fight the terror war. Should we then live in fear and lock ourselves in our armed homes and businesses, praying that we have enough firepower to win? No, no, no! It is still possible to turn the tide against this evil of terrorism. How? Victory starts with you. It starts with an army of one who has the passion and conviction that individuals can make a difference.

Why do I think one individual can make a difference? I not only have shelves filled with stories of others who have made a difference, but I personally experienced what one single soul can do when I got involved in halting the dismantling of preventive law enforcement in Los Angeles in 1981. There are tens and tens of millions of "ones" in this country who want a society where all people are truly free and able to practice the peaceful worship of their God. Most Americans have been so brainwashed that we believe we'll be protected by the government. We think we should merely be quiet, not make waves, and believe as we're told.

Further, the press in this country is so slanted to the left, so dismissive of the spiritual nature of the fight, that sometimes I wonder what the media's real motives are. Time after time in my twenty-five-plus years involved in the Middle East, I witnessed firsthand the biased American press portraying the Jews as aggressors and land grabbers. Meanwhile, the PLO and other terrorists could kill innocent civilians by the thousands, as they did in Lebanon, and our press raised not one question.

Finally, I see a media and culture that seems oblivious to the fact we are in what can only be described as a world war. As I write this, tens of thousands of Islamic militants across the globe are plotting the murder of Americans, Jews, Christians, and moderate Muslims. Their agents continue probing for weaknesses and maintain their surveillance of targets right here in America. Today, there are warnings about more hijackings, chemical attacks on subways and trains, attacks at shopping malls, and other high-profile events. But as we have seen in the past, the top media are more interested in a perverted, faded pop star, a murderous cheating husband, or whether Paris Hilton has what it takes to be a porn star or a farm girl.

We must fix our attention on what is truly important. We must not be distracted by the silly notions of what passes for fame in our culture. We must be firm, attentive, and insistent that our public officials do the job we elected them to do—to keep us and our children safe. Only when a unified people demand change will the necessary changes be made. But it all begins with one person. I'm determined to be a person like that. Won't you join me?

9/11 Wake-Up Call

I BELIEVE SEPTEMBER 11 was a cold, hard slap in the face. It was a wake-up call, and not only for the much-needed improvements in our intelligence-gathering capabilities; it was also a message that our very survival is at risk. We must come to grips with what is going on in the world, how we got to this place, and what we can do to turn the tide back to the values that God intended us to live by.

Some people might ask, "How can you be so sure we have another chance?" Let's look at the record. In the Old Testament, when people wanted to change their way of life and reverse the flood of evil that had come upon their countries and lives, every time—time after time, in fact—God always gave them another chance. Think of God's conversations with Noah and Abraham or how Isaiah made poetry out of God's joyful offering of renewed covenant. The book of Judges as well as 1 and 2 Kings are almost comical in depicting God repeatedly welcoming his people back after they scamper off. In the New Testament, what is Jesus' parable of the Prodigal Son if not a metaphor for God's willingness to run and greet our return? God says he is the same "yesterday, today, and forever." His Word is immutable, and he is no respecter of persons. What he did for the people in Bible times he will do for us. We can still change our situation, and I know we *want* to change our situation.

My desire to write this book stems in part from the questions and comments I receive from the thousands of people I have met when I speak on terrorism. People ask me, "What can I do? How can I make a difference?" Many offered money to support what I was doing. I don't want to discourage giving to worthy causes, but I must say that sometimes that's the easy way out for us: Give money and let someone else take care of it. Pay taxes and let the government and military take care of it. That won't work in this battle. We all have to do our part to stop this onslaught of evil. We all have the power of one.

Where do we start?

The first step is to know the true enemy. We must conclude and accept that terrorism, at its core, is an evil plot hatched by the deceiver, Satan. To classify the war on terrorism as the battle between good and evil is not a warped desire of religious zealots but a truth that has been hidden from us. Remember, our tendency is to put our heads down and ignore how the world is going to hell around us. We may think, *It doesn't affect me or mine. Just leave me alone and let me work as hard as I can to have more things to satisfy my desire for ease and fun.* If we don't recognize that this is fundamentally a spiritual battle, if we fool ourselves into thinking, *It has to do with political power, It's a culture clash,* or *They're just thugs,* we will fail. But if we understand the nature of the problem and recognize evil, we will have the lay of the battlefield.

Perhaps some people are put off by the religious aspect of what I am saying. Well, then, look at it this way: When somebody declares a religious war against you, *believe it!* The enemy has declared a *jihad.* He is acting on what he believes are the divine orders of his god: acting in his name, declaring his "greatness" while setting off bombs and slitting the throats of our citizens. In the 9/11 chapter, I asked what spirit God could put in man that he would go into a flaming building to rescue strangers, when every instinct says to flee. Here, I ask what spirit fills a man to cause him to gleefully destroy himself and hundreds of strangers by slamming into that building in the first place?

How then do we fight such a spirit, the spirit that fuels and fosters terrorism? With prayer. Pray for our nation and our leaders. We should pray "without ceasing" even if we don't see any immediate results. Remember, we are called only to pray; the results are up to God. Sometimes when we don't see quick results, we wear out and stop, thinking we aren't getting through, as if God's line can have a busy signal. God always hears and always acts. Another benefit is that prayer also focuses our own attention on whatever it is we're praying about.

One thing that diverts us from praying is not having sufficient faith in God. If our faith is low, how do we increase it? Before we can have faith in anyone, we must know him. My life of faith grows only when I obtain more knowledge and understanding about God, who he is, and how he works. God gives a very detailed record, the Bible, about his character, his life, and how he operates. If we spend time in the Bible, we will get to know who God is, come to trust in his Word, and know he will never deceive us. We will find, over time, that our faith has grown, little by little, with each circumstance we face. With each hurdle we overcome, the next one gets a little bigger, but our faith has also grown to enable us to overcome this higher obstacle. There is no shortcut to developing a lifestyle of faith and trust in our Creator, and faith will grow only as we commit ourselves to the discipline of daily time with God. Just as we take time to feed our bodies because our stomachs are yelling out for food, we must take time to feed our spirits. Why don't we feed our spirit with the same fervor we do our natural body? Too many times in our busy lives we ignore or just don't hear the hunger aches of our spirit. This must change if we are going to survive as a free people. September 11 told us this is the time to strengthen our spiritual life. It is the time to call on God to intercede. It is, as the gospel music classic shouts, "Prayin' Time."

Now that we've prayed, we're ready to fight, not only as spiritual warriors but as citizen warriors. The battle starts right in our own neighborhoods. We need to learn what local government is doing and what its stand is on preventive law enforcement. We need to know, elect, and then badger local officials to ensure they are keeping our communities on the right path. This applies to all levels of government. We must deal with the issues at each level that affect our security. Here are some examples of actions you can take on various levels:

- Personal: Are you alert? Have you trained your household?
- Local: Are your community's first responders properly equipped to handle trouble? Is there pressure on the city to cut the budget for preventive measures? What can you do to counteract that pressure?
- State: Is your governor leading your state's homeland security measures in a way that says he or she understands what this fight is about? If not, start to inform him or her—and the voters—of the facts.
- National: Are candidates serious about the war on terror, or are they using the issue only to score political points? Will you volunteer to help those who are serious?
- International: Are you aware of international terror groups and their surrogates? When you hear groups complain about U.S. policy, do you know the source of their funding?

Earlier in this book I related that when I got involved in helping to fight those who were trying to destroy preventive law enforcement and intelligence gathering in Los Angeles, the politicians chided us with, "Where have you people been?" They had only been hearing the shrill voices of the left-leaning extremists and not hearing from "We, the People," the 95 percent who thought pretty much the same and wanted the same things from our government. From that initial start with one voice, the chorus became thousands and we saved intelligence gathering in Los Angeles. When the issue is terrorism, never let it be asked of you, "Where have you been?" Take heart. Have faith that you, too, can be the one who starts a landslide in your community, a landslide that could have a national impact.

If you need some tips on how to start investigating various levels of government, send me an e-mail at plittle@wc detective.com and I'll help you. And once you've learned the necessary facts, your next step is to start letting your elected officials know how you feel about terrorism. Patiently and in a balanced way, let them know the source of terrorism. Tell them the only way to fight terrorism is to prevent it, and to prevent attacks we need strong intelligence gathering to know in advance what the terrorists have planned.

Our focus in the intelligence-gathering arena needs to be on human assets, but we also need spy satellites and other electronic means. We need to infiltrate the terror networks. We need to get our message into schools and societies that train their youth to hate and kill us. We started the decline in human assets years ago, and on the Clinton watch it was disabled so effectively that 9/11 was a cakewalk for al-Qaeda. There were many reasons for dismantling a system of agents on the ground. One was the demise of the Soviet Union, which convinced many officials we were past the days of a global threat. Others saw intelligence gathering as infringement on citizens' rights. This reasoning has been used all over the world by leftists whose true goal is to turn governments into a Socialist club controlled by a few. The cry of "spying on the innocent citizens" has been used very effectively by our enemies to mobilize well-meaning populations against their governments and disband intelligence units. Informed and educated people are powerful people. If you are aware of the tactics, you won't be deceived by them. If you hear this sort of rhetoric in your communities, go into action. Get on the phone, call the local leaders handling the issue, write letters, and make noise. It does make a difference. If the onslaught goes forward, contact the press, write letters to the editor, flood talk radio, and, if necessary, form a citizens' committee and call a press conference. The facts are on your side. We can't simply leave our security in the hands of righteous men and women in government. They need our help and support.

We Americans have a history of getting busy with our own lives and not getting involved in our government or election processes. When 20 percent—or sometimes less—can elect our leaders, then we are in trouble. In fact, such slim turnouts can allow fringe candidates with devoted followings to sneak into office. Consider this: Moammar Ghadafi's son, who has been assuming increasing power in Libya, suggested that radical Islam has a better chance of success in the Western world if it emulates the Jewish model of working from inside the system. He thinks Islamists can run for office and win, thus getting into a better position to gain power. Extremists like his father are easy to spot; it's the radicals in moderate clothing who pose the greater danger.

On the other hand, the 2004 presidential election displayed the power of the vote to express majority opinion and gives hope that this might be a sign of an awaking public.

I believe the reason our country is so far along the road in risking our freedoms is because each one of us is not doing his or her part as a citizen. Having become accustomed to all the freedoms we enjoy, we sometimes act as if we expect the government to do it all. Still, I believe there is hope for America if we, the uninvolved people, become involved and let our voices be heard. Become an activist; it's not a bad word. Just because some activists promote bad causes doesn't mean we can't be active for the good of all.

It is imperative that we understand what is at stake in this battle against terrorism. I don't want to be melodramatic or overly repetitive, but I submit to you again that the existence of the world as we know it could be at stake. I believe I hear the cry from the heart of God himself, wanting to rally a force of good to oppose this force of evil. I sense the cry "Who will hear? Who will stand up?" Indeed, who will stand in the gap to raise a standard against this violence that could propel us toward the worst war we can imagine?

We must heed this call to blend our voices of reason and demand our leaders follow a path of prevention so as to not allow terrorism to divide the world along religious lines. As I stated in an earlier chapter, I am concerned terrorism could be the vehicle that causes the United States to remove itself from the Middle East and the protection of Israel. If this should happen, the stage could be set for powers to move against Israel and bring about the unthinkable. We have within us the power and ability to be those who rise up, get involved, and push back this evil that wants to destroy us.

The dark minds behind the terrorist groups expect you to be a soft and easy target. Americans, they truly think, have all the luxuries in the world and have been pampered so much and for so long they expect things to be comfortable. They assume we'll become disinterested and discouraged if the process gets too difficult. And, admittedly, there is a segment of our society that is soft, especially when it comes to moral issues affecting the fabric of our country. When we have forces within our own country pushing the concept that there is no God and no fixed moral code, when we have an increasingly secular media preaching the message "Do what you want, live for today, and get away with all you can," it's no wonder the terrorists think our society is a target ripe for conquest.

We've seen throughout this book that terrorism is motivated by an evil that aims to conquer us. But, as Yogi Berra used to say, "It ain't over 'til it's over." And that's what I believe about this battle against terrorism. We are in a fight, a bloody fight destined to see many more casualties. But be of good cheer, as Jesus said. The victory is ours.

Let's break out of the mold of passivism and become activists for good. I have so much hope for our world and country, and I have faith in you. Together, we can push the terrorist groups into a deep pit from which they cannot escape. The future of America and the world is in our hands—not Osama bin Laden's, Hezbollah's, or even the hands of Lucifer himself. But we must take the action necessary to remove the ability for evil and its agents to act.

Today, I am working to mobilize citizens across America to stand up against the onslaught of those who would destroy our freedoms. If you are ready to join us—and if you've read this far I know you are—e-mail me at plittle@wcdetective.com for ways you can help in your community. I pray you will join me. Believe me, it's not too late.